FINDING LOST THINGS

DAN McCOLLAM

PROPHETICCOMPANY.COM

Copyright © 2020 Dan McCollam

All rights reserved.

All Scripture quotations, unless otherwise indicated, are taken from the Holy Bible, New International Version®, NIV®. Copyright ©1973, 1978, 1984, 2011 by Biblica, Inc.™ Used by permission of Zondervan. All rights reserved worldwide. The "NIV" and "New International Version" are trademarks registered in the United States Patent and Trademark Office by Biblica, Inc.™ Some Scripture taken from *The Message*. Copyright © 1993, 1994, 1995, 1996, 2000, 2001, 2002. Used by permission of NavPress Publishing Group. Some Scripture taken from the NEW AMERICAN STANDARD BIBLE®, Copyright © 1960, 1962, 1963, 1968, 1971, 1972, 1973, 1975, 1977, 1995 by The Lockman Foundation. Used by permission. Some Scripture taken from *Holy Bible*, New Living Translation, copyright © 1996, 2004, 2015 by Tyndale House Foundation. Used by permission of Tyndale House Publishers, Inc., Carol Stream, Illinois 60188. All rights reserved.

Cover art by bravoboy at 99Designs.com.

Published by Dan McCollam in cooperation with Prophetic Company.

ISBN: 9798687385480

CONTENTS

Introduction   v

1. The Heart of the Matter   1
2. Rest Or Stress   7
3. Watch Your Declarations   13
4. You're Being Followed   19
5. Divine Recall   25
6. Sensitivity Training   31
7. Finding With Hearing   39
8. Finding With Seeing   53
9. Finding With Knowing   61
10. Signs and Wonders   71
11. Angels On Assignment   81
12. Teamwork   89
13. Dream Or Night Vision   97
14. Mapping Methods   103
15. Mystical Methods   109
16. 3rd Heaven Seeking   117
17. Perseverance and Variance of Methods   121
18. The Ethics of Searching   129
19. Putting It All Together   141

Notes   145

INTRODUCTION

Everyone loses things. It is precisely because loss is common to all mankind that many of us have learned to accept losing as a normal part of life. We learn to embrace loss. But is a life of loss normal? Does God intend for mankind to live with a certain inevitability of loss? For the answer to that question, we should begin with a working definition of the word "loss." The dictionary defines loss as "the act of losing possession, the harm or privation resulting from loss or separation, an instance of losing."[1] So, loss is a state of losing, separation, and harm. Doesn't sound like God to me.

Yet, God is personally familiar with loss and separation. Bible history tells us that one third of the angels God created rebelled and had to be removed from their position. Loss and separation. Man rebelled and threw the whole of creation into a state of separation from God. Loss, separation, and losing

INTRODUCTION

appear to be part of God's story as well as our own. If you stop here, then you might be tempted to confirm loss as inevitable and live with a certain amount of hopelessness. But God is also a finder. His very nature and mission is to seek and to save that which is lost. (Luke 19:10) Before there existed any loss or separation, God designed a plan to find and restore that which would be lost. He predetermined a reconciled outcome —a happy ending. (Revelation 13:8) Having preconceived a story of redemption, God wrote mankind into His happy ending and gave His sons and daughters the ability to live as restorers and reconcilers. Here are a couple of scriptures that talk about your part in the redemption story:

> 1 Corinthians 3:5-6
> Not that we are competent in ourselves to claim anything for ourselves, but our competence comes from God. He has made us competent as ministers of a new covenant—not of the letter but of the Spirit; for the letter kills, but the Spirit gives life.

> 2 Corinthians 5:18-19
> All this is from God, who reconciled us to himself through Christ and gave us the ministry of reconciliation: that God was reconciling the world to himself in Christ, not counting people's sins against them. And he has committed to us the message of reconciliation.

INTRODUCTION

God reconciled the world to Himself. He healed its lost state through the death, burial, and resurrection of Jesus Christ and then gave mankind competence as restorers and reconcilers. The good news is that because of God's love, work, and nature, nothing and no one needs to stay lost or separated. We join in God's mission to seek and save that which is lost. This applies most definitely and gloriously to the area of salvation and redemption of human lives, but finding lost things is an additional benefit to friendship with God.

In these pages, I will share supernatural ways to find lost things, ways which are accessible through your friendship with God. God speaks to all of us in many different ways. The challenge is never in getting God to speak because God is always speaking; the challenge is to recognize all the ways that God is speaking. God is certainly speaking to us about our lost things; we must only learn how to recognize it.

Each chapter is designed to help you recognize and respond to a specific way that God transmits spiritual intelligence in the ministry of redemption and reconciliation. Each concept will explore simple and practical Bible truths that introduce a new way that God could be speaking into your circumstance. The teachings are followed by clearly marked activation steps for finding lost things.

In the process of writing this book, I put out an invitation to my social media community to share their

INTRODUCTION

"finder's stories" with me. Friends and followers quickly answered with fun and simple stories that correlated surprisingly well with the main points of each chapter already written. In collecting these stories, something else wonderful and unexpected happened. Together, our insights and testimonies created this quantum global story of redemption that was greater and louder than my own thoughts and observations. The book took on a global voice, making it clear that these finding graces are available to anyone and everyone who believes.

As you read, you may notice that I often omitted the word "the" before referring to Holy Spirit. I think it is important in this book to emphasize His personhood. Many believers subconsciously think of the Spirit merely as an expression of God rather than a full member of the godhead. Partnership with the person of Holy Spirit is foundational to this exploration of supernatural ways to find lost things, so I chose to retain the word "the" when it was used in a scripture reference or quote but otherwise omit it to emphasize the sweetness of our fellowship with God in the midst of our searching.

It is my hope that this book will serve you in finding lost things. I also desire that these stories and insights will inspire you to know the riches and depths of God's grace and love on a whole new level. May your friendship and fellowship with God deepen and grow. Finally, may these simple thoughts and stories build in you a conviction of the absolute redemption of all things created and restored through Christ Jesus and may you join this global story as a finder and redeemer.

1
THE HEART OF THE MATTER

FINDING LOST THINGS starts with daring to believe that God loves you and He cares about your lost stuff. Do you know that God cares about lost things? Many people don't know or believe this when it comes to their own lost things.

We can see God's heart for the lost in the declared mission of Jesus Christ:

> Luke 19:10
> For the Son of Man came to seek and save that which is lost.

Look carefully. The text does not say that Jesus came to save only lost souls but all things that are lost. It is because of the mission of Jesus Christ that I believe there is an anointing attached to everything and everyone that is lost. Jesus came with a heart for the lost. He cares about the lost and fallen state of all creation.

Look at the tender care expressed for creation in this passage:

> Matthew 10:29-30
> Are not two sparrows sold for a penny? Yet not one of them will fall to the ground outside your Father's care. And even the very hairs of your head are numbered.

Sometimes we are under the wrong idea that God won't help us find something lost because He doesn't care, or He is busy with more important issues, or He is against us having physical possessions in the first place so why would He help us find it. These are all wrong ideas that contribute to the mire of unbelief blocking the flow of finder's grace.

God is not against you owning stuff; He is against stuff owning you. He doesn't want your identity, your value, or your joy sourced from owning temporal things, but He is not against you enjoying things. God enjoys things. In the beginning of the Bible narrative, we see God enjoying what He made. The Bible pictures God carefully creating each detail of the physical universe and then standing back and admiring what He made and calling it "good." (Genesis 1:10, 12, 18, 21, 25, 31) By calling creation "good," God expressed His joy in everything created. God is not against you owning things; He Himself is an owner. Look with me in scripture at the description of God's assets.

> Psalm 24:1
> The earth is the LORD's and everything in it,
> the world, and all who live in it.

Owning everything in the earth doesn't make God materialistic or shallow. He cares for each thing He owns. Because He cares for what He owns, He has a heart for what is lost.

The parables of Luke 15 demonstrate God's love for lost things. When Jesus expressed His mission of seeking and saving the lost, He followed the statement by three crafted stories about finding the lost. First was the story of a woman's lost coin. Next came the story of the good shepherd leaving the ninety-nine sheep to find one sheep that was lost. Finally, He shared the story of two lost sons. Though there are certainly deeper theological implications to each of these parables, the simple truth revealed in them is certainly that God cares about lost coins, lost sheep, and lost people. God cares about lost stuff and believing it is so makes room for spiritual intel which leads to recovering what is lost.

I met a woman who was grieving deeply over her lost pet. She was so embarrassed to admit it. She would say, "I know there are more important things in the world, and I'm embarrassed at how much I'm grieving, but since my husband died, this pet has been my closest companion." She was afraid of appearing petty or materialistic. The hurting woman wasn't convinced that God cared about her lost animal or her broken heart. That's so sad. Unbelief or ignorance concerning God's care for you and what is lost is a data blocker. The wellspring of spiritual intelligence flows from a heart drenched in the love of the Father for you and for all His creation. God cares about lost things and He cares about you.

Each member of the Godhead is truly with you in your search. Look at the following passage with me.

> 2 Corinthians 13:14
> May the grace of the LORD Jesus Christ, and
> the love of God, and the fellowship of the Holy
> Spirit be with you all.

This is an amazing demonstration of how much God cares. God and all His virtues are with you right now! Grace is the empowering agent of God to help you do through Christ what you could not do on your own just a moment before. So, the grace possessed by the person of Jesus Christ is with you in your search. That's a lot of grace! Next, the love of God the Father is with you reminding you that God cares about you and your lost stuff. The love of the Father will accompany and empower you on every step of this finder's mission. Finally, you have fellowship with Holy Spirit. It is this fellowship with Holy Spirit that gives you access to supernatural intelligence. God cares enough to go with you in your search and provide for you through his own person all that you need to find that which is lost. All persons of the godhead are with you in this ministry of reconciliation and redemption. With all this divine help, you can surely find your lost thing.

ACTIVATE God's Care

1. BUILD A TRUST BRIDGE. Let God's love and care become a trust bridge for the flow of spiritual intelligence. Build your trust bridge by meditating on the following passage:

> Proverbs 3:5-6
> Trust in the LORD will all your heart and lean not on your own understanding; in all your ways acknowledge him, and he will direct your path.

2. MAKE A CONSCIOUS SHIFT. Shift your consciousness from self-effort and natural understanding to supreme and divine intelligence. Cast your care on Him and focus on how much He loves and cares for you. Here is another scripture to meditate on and memorize:

> 1 Peter 5:7
> Cast all your anxiety on him because He cares for you.

3. PRACTICE AWARENESS. Practice awareness of the presence of the Godhead and of His virtues in your life. Confess with me: The grace of Jesus on me makes all things possible. The love of the Father for me comforts and strengthens me in my search. The fellowship of Holy Spirit in me gives me access to supernatural intelligence. Thank you, God, that you are in me and with me.

2
REST OR STRESS

LOSING SOMETHING CAN BE STRESSFUL, especially if it is time sensitive. Perhaps you have lost your passport, and you need to travel soon; or maybe you lost the work ID to get into your office. Most people at some time in their life have experienced the stress of losing car keys when already late for an appointment. I get it. Loss is stressful. But stress can be a data-blocker. The more you stress, the more the answers will elude you.

Eternal intelligence doesn't function well in an atmosphere of demands. You won't unwrap eternal gifts of supernatural guidance in a finite cardboard box of stress and impatience. Fear of loss and the accompanying stress are antithetical to the nature of God and His kingdom. God's kingdom is composed of righteousness, peace, and joy in the Holy Spirit. (Romans 14:17) If you know Jesus as your Lord and Savior, His kingdom dwells within you. (Luke 17:21) That means you have the power to choose to live either from the outside in or from the inside out. You can allow the outside environment and circumstances to set the state of your inward attitudes, or you can let the Kingdom atmosphere within you overtake your external environment and rule over stressful circumstances. Choosing peace is a key to unlocking spiritual intel that leads to recovering what is lost. Jesus made a wonderful promise describing the kind of peace He wanted you to have:

> John 14:27
> Peace I leave with you; My peace I give to you; not as the world gives do I give to you. Do not let your heart be troubled, nor let it be fearful.

Do you see it? It says, "Do not let...," indicating that you have a choice. Stress is not the inevitable outcome of troubling circumstances and loss; stress is a choice of kingdom rule. In your temporary loss, you must choose which kingdom you will live from and relate to. You hold the reigns to your heart's response. "Do not let" trouble guide the reigns of your hunt for lost things. "Do not let" fear be the operating system of your search engine. Give stress a "cease and desist order" from the throne room of God and His kingdom within you.

Peace is a fascinating principle with a direct application to finding lost things. Inferior earthly thinking says that peace is found through understanding. It reasons the more you know and understand the more peace you will have. While it is true that there is something satisfying in the discovery of true wisdom, knowledge, and revelation, those born from above by God's Spirit discover that peace precedes understanding. You are more likely to find understanding through peace than you are to find peace through understanding. So, you must often choose peace when you don't understand in order to actually experience a favorable outcome and open the flow of divine intelligence. Here is one of the places you can find this principle reflected in the living and active word of God:

> Philippians 4:6-7
> Do not be anxious about anything, but in every situation, by prayer and petition, with thanksgiving, present your request to God. And the peace of God, which transcends all understanding, will guard your hearts and minds in Christ Jesus.

Because peace is foundational to God's kingdom, we must choose peace in order to access eternal intelligence. Choosing stress will release a revelation repellant. I know, it seems hard at first to "chill out" when you are under real time constraints, but it is still a productive choice. Scripture tells us that anxiety in your heart can weight it down. (Proverbs 12:25) It says that hope deferred can even make the heart sick. (Proverbs 13:12) A heavy, weighed down, sickened heart is not a great starting ground for the reception of spiritual information. Supernatural intelligence flows in and out of a healthy heart. That is why we are given this command:

> Proverbs 4:23
> Watch over your heart with all diligence, for from it flow the springs of life.

You must get your heart healthy by casting off anxiety and renewing hope. Break agreement with worry, fear of loss, and hope deferred. That is, break agreement with all forms of hopelessness.

Another thing to consider is what allowing yourself to be overwhelmed with frustration sows into the atmosphere around you. Choosing against peace creates an atmosphere of stress in your home or work environment. In this atmosphere, people are often hurt. Harsh and careless words flow from stress-choosers, striking and wounding innocent bystanders. I hate to admit how many times I have done things this way. We all must ask ourselves, "Is this really how I want to live? Is this attitude and behavior helping me find anything?"

The God who cares for you beyond comprehension and who absolutely knows where your lost thing sits is humbly waiting in the wings for your acknowledgment. As one who seldom imposes His will on others, Holy Spirit is quietly anticipating your invitation. It's like the picture of a child throwing a tantrum when he can't find his toy; and when he finally asks mom, she tells him exactly where it is. So, are you done yet? Are you done with self-effort and stress? Are you done leaning on your own understanding? Are you ready to take the reins of your heart and hand them to the Prince of Peace?

ACTIVATE Peace

1. BREAK AGREEMENT WITH STRESS. Make a declaration with me, "Stress, you are not my friend or helper. I break agreement with you and your ways. I step into eternal peace and hand the reins of my heart and this search for what is lost over to God. Prince of Peace, please guard and guide my life and my search for I trust in You."

2. STAY AT PEACE. Prove your peace for a bit. Don't stress if the answer doesn't come right away. Remember, we are choosing peace over understanding in order to center ourselves in Kingdom reality. You can't leverage peace in order to get answers. You must enter its rest to taste of its fruit. Embrace the atmosphere and virtue of peace.

3. CLEAN UP MESSES. Don't forget to clean up any messes you've made. Is there any relational clean-up to do? Did you launch any stress bombs or throw a little tantrum before choosing peace? If so, go back and humbly repent. Say something like "I'm sorry I acted like that and said things that were hurtful or untrue. I was frustrated at my loss, but you are precious to me.

Please forgive me. I am choosing now to walk in peace, and you can call me on it if I do otherwise."

4. RULE THE ATMOSPHERE. Finally, let the Kingdom within rule the atmosphere around. Breathe in and out deeply for a moment while you are exchanging atmospheres. Let the Prince of Peace sit on the throne of your heart and let your stressful thoughts and frustration go. Enter the transcendence of His peace.

Your heart and spirit are the transfer points of spiritual intelligence that lead to supernatural finding. Guard them carefully to ensure the unrestricted flow of divine wisdom. Let peace rule and reign in your heart.

3
WATCH YOUR DECLARATIONS

YOUR SPIRITUAL GIFTS must past through the gateway of your faith. No matter how big or strong your gifts or graces are, they must pass through the funnel of the size of your faith and expectation. As the Holy Book reveals, each gifting works not only according to the size of the gift (Ephesians 4:7, 1 Corinthians 12:11) but also in proportion to your faith. (Romans 12:3, 6)

Calling an object "lost" or "stolen" can subtly imply that the item is either gone forever or will be extremely challenging to find. That's not a good starting place.

Here is another important spiritual principle: Your experience rises to the level of your declarations. What has your declaration been concerning your lost thing? Have you perhaps cursed your ability to find it by unwittingly uttering careless declarations? That's what happens when we say things like "I can't find it anywhere;" "I have searched everywhere and can't find it;" "I guess it's gone forever;" "I will never find this thing;" or "I guess it's time to just let it go." The problem with anti-faith declarations is that they hinder the flow of supernatural intelligence.

Lori, from Northern California, learned this lesson when looking for her lost keys. Here is her finder's story:

> *I rent a studio suite with kitchen access in a home. To access the kitchen, I use a separate entrance with my key. One day, after preparing an artichoke, I was frantically looking for my key. My words were, "God! I can't find my key! I don't want to tell my landlord I lost the key! God, help me find my key!" For fifteen minutes my mantra was, "I lost my key!" I looked everywhere, even in places I hadn't been, just in case. I even dug through the garbage, which was not pretty since I just threw away a chicken. Yuck! Still, my mantra, "I can't find my key! God, please help!"*
>
> *It was then that I realized the words I was using. I laughed and said, "I find everything I look for!" Instantly, and without hesitation, my hand went to the little pocket where I had stuffed my key, just to be safe! I laughed out loud when I realized that our words carry so much power. In just the little things—like finding a key—God wants us to craft our*

words to be a blessing. When we partner with Him, miracles happen!

Amen, Lori! I love Lori's declaration, "I find everything I look for!" That's a helpful finder's key because our words are important. Jesus used words to shape worlds as He literally spoke the universe into existence. Look how the psalmist beautifully frames this truth.

Psalm 33:6-9
By the word of the Lord the heavens were made, their starry host by the breath of his mouth. He gathers the waters of the sea into jars; he puts the deep into storehouses. Let all the earth fear the Lord; let all the people of the world revere him. For he spoke, and it came to be; he commanded, and it stood firm.

Because we are made in God's image (Genesis 1:26-27), our words can carry creative force to shape or break our reality. One of the wisest kings of history said, "The power of life and death are in the tongue; and those who love it will eat its fruits." (Proverbs 18:21) Judging by your declarations, what fruit are you eating? How do you like the taste of frustration? How is that fruit of despair working out? Are you enjoying that "never-ever" burger you are gnawing on? Why don't you switch to the fillet mignon of a faith declaration?

Remember that God knows where your lost thing is. As a matter of fact, scripture tells us that nothing in all of creation is hidden from His sight. (Hebrews 4:13) Paul's letter to the Corinthian church tells us that Holy Spirit can search and know everything.

> 1 Corinthians 2:9-10
> However, as it is written: "What no eye has seen, what no ear has heard, and what no human mind has conceived" –the things God has prepared for those who love him—these are the things God has revealed to us by his Spirit. The Spirit searches all things, even the deep things of God.

Holy Spirit is a seeker. He searches out everything and reveals it to us who love Him. Why don't we take advantage of that? Why do we trust in our own thoughts and abilities to find what is missing? Let's abdicate that throne and put the One who already knows and sees everything upon it. True seeking should start with trusting and enthroning the greatest Seeker of them all and making declarations that reflect that trust. The words of your mouth form the gate of your faith. Changing your declarations can help apprehend a supernatural result.

Let's expand that faith gate even more using the tool of thanksgiving. Did you know that grumbling and complaining are like the praise and worship of the kingdom of darkness? In the same way that God inhabits or is enthroned upon the praises of His people (Psalm 22:3), the kingdom of darkness is enthroned through grumbling, murmuring, and complaining. The word murmur in Hebrew comes from a root word *luwn* which means "to stop, stay permanently, to abide, lodge, or tether." When you complain about your lost thing or murmur about losing it, you are lodging in loss and renting a room in the flea-bag motel of unbelief. Don't reserve a room of regrets. Displace your complaints with thanksgiving. The psalmist David shows us the entry point to eternal intelligence.

> Psalm 100:4
> Enter his gates with thanksgiving and his courts with praise; give thanks to him and praise his name.

If you want to cut the tether of earthly limitations, then do it with a heart of thanksgiving and a declaration of praise. Praise and thanksgiving swing open the gates of both heaven and earth, making room for supernatural results. What you say and declare about your lost thing is important.

ACTIVATE Faith-Filled Declarations

1. BREAK AGREEMENT. Break agreement with any hopeless announcement and with former declarations that defined your missing item as "lost." You might want to say something like "Father, forgive me. I repent of saying things like 'I'll never find (name what you are looking for).' I don't believe I'll never find it."

2. REOPEN THE DOOR TO YOUR FAITH GATE. Make declarations like "Father, You know all things and search all things. (2 Corinthians 2:9-10) Nothing in all creation is hidden from Your sight. (Hebrews 4:13) You have given me the mind of Christ and the fellowship of Holy Spirit. (1 Corinthians 2:16, 2 Corinthians 13:14) I am confident we will find and uncover this by Your divine intelligence."

3. OPEN THE GATES OF POSSIBILITY. Widen them using thanksgiving and praise. You might use words that sound something like this: "Thank you, Father, that You care for me. Thank you that You care about lost things. Thank you that You know right where my item is, and You have given me the mind of Christ to uncover it."

4. NOW, SET YOUR HEART IN AGREEMENT. Agree with these statements and let a new confidence enter your heart and mind to discover together with God your hidden thing. Reframe your mindset from your item being lost or stolen to simply being hidden or misplaced. Make a declaration of faith like Lori's: "Thank you, God, that in Christ I find everything I look for."

4

YOU'RE BEING FOLLOWED

DID YOU KNOW you are being followed? Yep. It's true. The culprits are found in one of the most famous and dearly loved Psalms in the Bible. The twenty-third psalm pictures a Good Shepherd leading us with provision and protection. The psalm closes with this powerful promise revealing the virtues following us.

> Psalm 23:6
> Surely your goodness and mercy will follow me all the days of my life, and I will dwell in the house of the LORD forever.

Goodness and mercy will follow you all the days of your life. Why are these virtues following you? Let me compare it to an old American game show called "Who Wants to Be a Millionaire?" Contestants were asked fourteen multiple-choice trivia questions. A string of correct answers could land them a prize of up to one million dollars. Along the journey, the contestants were granted help tools called "lifelines." My favorite lifeline was called "phone-a-friend." The contestant had the opportunity to make one phone call to a person whom they thought might know the answer. In searching for your lost item, have you "phoned-the-friends" of goodness and mercy? That is why they are following you. These virtues of our Father have been graciously assigned to accompany each of us on life's journey.

I have personally experienced the power of calling on goodness and mercy. Here is one of my finder's stories:

> *Once while returning home on an airplane, I was uncomfortable sitting on the wallet in my back pocket. Feeling rather confined for space and not wanting to bend over and stick it in the backpack at my feet, I tucked it into the seat pocket in front of me, quite sure that I would remember to retrieve it before I left. As you have likely figured out, I didn't realize I had left my wallet full of credit cards, essential ID, and a few hundred bucks until I had exited security and collected my luggage from baggage claim. Rushing to the luggage help counter I asked if the plane could be stopped. Unfortunately, the attendant informed me that the plane was already in the air crossing the length of the United States from the west coast to the east coast. In these days of identity theft and credit card fraud, I knew I had been*

left vulnerable by my forgetfulness. I made several phone calls to the lost-and-found department of the airlines, going through all the proper channels in hopes of recovering my lost treasures in a timely and safe way.

When it seemed clear that my customer service support options were coming to an end, I "phoned-the-friends" of goodness and mercy to help me. "Father," I prayed, "You said your goodness and mercy would follow me. Let your goodness and mercy follow my wallet until it is safely recovered and the contents returned. Let some good and merciful passenger or flight attendant take the time to return it."

I wish I had prayed that prayer earlier. My wallet had racked up several frequent flyer miles before I had taken the wise step to cry out in prayer, and therefore, someone had already helped themselves to the cash. But shortly after my prayer, a good Samaritan (Luke 10:33cf) had mercy on me and turned my wallet and its remaining contents into airport authorities. The most important things —my driver's license and credit cards—were returned without any misuse whatsoever. Calling on goodness and mercy were the keys to this safe return.

I have heard people say, "Humans are basically good. So, you can trust in the goodness of others for the return of your lost things." Forgive me for saying so, but I'm not wanting to gamble my faith on human goodness alone. The theology of human goodness or badness is a conversation and doctrinal rabbit hole way beyond the purpose of this book. But when it comes to this subject, I do know this: "Surely, goodness and mercy follow me all the days of my life." Regardless of human graces and limitations, I can call for the support of the heavenly virtues of goodness and mercy to manifest even in unexpected places. With this kind of faith, goodness and mercy may even show up in someone who is not known for demonstrating those virtues, like a thief or a total stranger.

The Falig family lives in Chicago, Illinois. Here is the story of how they experienced the power of calling in a Good Samaritan.

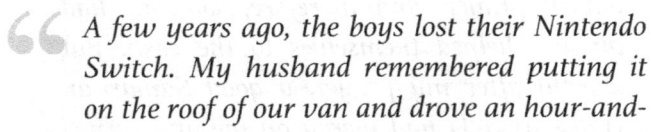

> *A few years ago, the boys lost their Nintendo Switch. My husband remembered putting it on the roof of our van and drove an hour-and-a-half before realizing what had happened. We prayed and prayed as that is an expensive item that could not be easily replaced. My husband posted online that it was missing.*
>
> *A few days later, a complete stranger somehow saw the plea and called us saying he had found it. The game system had flown off*

the roof of the car but was in perfect condition as though nothing had happened.

This Falig family story is surely a testimony of goodness and mercy. It is also a testimony of doing due diligence. Divinely finding your lost item does not negate the fact that it is still likely to be turned into the lost-and-found, the front desk, or a police department. Have you checked there? The dad in this story posted a notice in the local newspaper. He did due diligence. You should keep checking in with those types of places and making the appropriate calls.

Trusting the supernatural for finding your lost item does not disqualify human involvement on your part or on the part of someone else. Human vessels can serve as your secret agents of goodness and mercy. Recruit Good Samaritans in the Spirit by calling them into your circumstances and do the appropriate follow up.

ACTIVATE Goodness and Mercy

1. CALL IN GOODNESS AND MERCY. If your item was lost or stolen outside of your protected boundaries, then I recommend phoning the friends of goodness and mercy as soon as possible. Pray a prayer similar to mine: "Father, I call for Your goodness and mercy to follow me and manifest as a Good Samaritan."

2. **NEXT, OPEN YOUR HEART.** Open your heart and your hope to the goodness and mercy of God showing up in people and in your circumstances through divine intervention.

3. **DO YOUR PART.** Remember, it's still wisdom to perform due diligence like checking with the lost-and-found or putting an ad in the paper. Human beings can be and most likely will be a part of God's divine provision.

5
DIVINE RECALL

IT'S ANNOYING TO MISPLACE SOMETHING, but it is even more so if you feel responsible as the one who lost it. Add to this the pressure cooker of trying to remember where you left or lost the item, and you've got a stew of frustration. When it comes to recall, has it ever seemed to you that the more you try to remember where you left your lost thing, the farther your thoughts run from you? Don't you wish you possessed a mind scanner or security camera that could just replay your thoughts and actions? We have something like that available to us in the person of Holy Spirit.

As we learned earlier, Holy Spirit thoroughly knows your thoughts and actions. The Book of John describes Him as a Helper and Advocate who will remind us of everything Jesus said. (John 14:26) It's not a stretch to believe that Holy Spirit has the power to remind us of our own thoughts and actions. You might have already tried memory exercises, but did you do them in intentional connection and harmony with the One who knows and searches all things? (1 Corinthians 2:10-11)

Revealing thoughts and mysteries is not just something God can do; it is related to one of His names. In the Book of Daniel, God is presented through the prophet as the Revealer of Mysteries. (Daniel 2:47) God revealed to Daniel the exact details of someone else's thoughts in a night dream. Look at a brief excerpt from that amazing story:

> Daniel 2:27-28
> Daniel answered before the king and said, "As for the mystery about which the king has inquired, neither wise men, conjurers, magicians, nor diviners are able to declare it to the king. However, there is a God in heaven who reveals mysteries, and He has made known to King Nebuchadnezzar what will take place in the latter days. This was your dream and the visions in your mind while on your bed."

Talk about a human having the divine ability to know thoughts; God made the king's hidden night thoughts available to Daniel for divine recall. Now if God has a proven record of knowing and revealing someone's thoughts and His name is Revealer of Mysteries, don't you believe He can certainly help you re-live and remember your own thoughts? Maureen from Western Australia believes it. She experienced the power and blessing of divine recall as recounted here in her finder's story:

> *I had misplaced a recipe book that I was interested in looking at. I looked in all the usual places. After quite some time that day, I had this clear picture in my mind's eye of me putting it in a suitcase for safe keeping. I went to the suitcase and immediately found the book and was wonderfully awed by this amazing experience. It was like a gift from God to realize He was interested in helping me with this seemingly small issue.*

That's great for Maureen, but perhaps you are asking, "How is that information transferred back to me?" The ancient biblical writings of King David might provide a key. In his Psalms, David declared his understanding that God knew all his ways and he invited God to search and know his thoughts.

> Psalm 139:1-3, 23
> You have searched me, Lord, and you know me.
> You know when I sit and when I rise; you
> perceive my thoughts from afar. You discern my
> going out and my lying down; you are familiar
> with all my ways...Search me, God, and know
> my heart, test me and know my anxious
> thoughts.

Have you invited the partnership of Holy Spirit, the Revealer of Mysteries, or have you just thrown up a prayer or two out of frustration? Some people's prayers seem more like a "Hail Mary" than a real prayer. If you haven't heard the expression "Hail Mary" outside of Catholicism, let me explain. In American grid-iron football there is a play nicknamed a "Hail Mary." Originally the expression described any sort of desperation play with a low probability of success. It usually consisted of a long pass at the end of the game or just before half-time as one last desperate attempt to score.[1]

The metaphor of a "Hail Mary" prayer is that tendency of believers to try everything we know to do first and then finally throw up a prayer as a last resort. I'm shocked by how many people pray that way. I'm also disappointed when I catch myself doing it. Too often, we pray this way with little expectation that anything will happen. But "Hey," we reason, "it's worth a try." If we don't really expect an answer or prioritize the divine in the process, then we shouldn't get mad at God when we don't receive help. Unfortunately, after praying without faith, people often use the lack of answered prayer to reinforce their own unbelief by responding to themselves, "I knew that wouldn't work." Even worse is to whisper to God, "I knew You wouldn't help." Divine recall and the revealing of mysteries does not happen through this kind of prayer.

The Book of James shows the lack of effectiveness in this kind of prayer.

> James 1:5-7
> If any of you lacks wisdom, you should ask God, who gives generously to all without finding fault, and it will be given to you. But when you ask, you must believe and not doubt. Because the one who doubts is like a wave of the sea, blown and tossed by the wind. That person should not expect to receive anything from the Lord.

Praying without faith makes you sound more like a beggar than a believer. But that is not what or who you are!

Believe in God's nature. When you pray for wisdom and for the searching of Holy Spirit, you must start from a place of believing in the nature of God as a generous giver. Look at the verse again and meditate on its sweet flavor. "You should ask God, who gives generously to all without finding fault, and it will be given to you." (James 1:5) God is not a faultfinder; He's not looking for a loophole or a reason to not answer your prayer. God loves to give wisdom, insight, and divine recall to those who are truly seeking His assistance. He gives generously to everyone. It's important to believe that things happen when you pray and ask from a place of true faith and expectancy. Divine recall is available to you from the Generous Giver and Revealer of Mysteries.

. . .

ACTIVATE Divine Recall

1. ASK FOR DIVINE RECALL. Rest in His presence for a moment. Focus on His goodness and generosity. Dismiss all ideas of disqualification or faultfinding. Set your expectation on receiving answers with the help of this great Mystery Revealer. Close your eyes and ask for divine recall. You might say something like this, "Holy Spirit, I know that you search all things and know all things, even my thoughts. You watched all my actions and steps. I am having trouble remembering where I left this item. Bring the memories back I pray in Jesus' name."

2. PRACTICE DIVINE RECALL. Now begin to picture your last contact with this item. In your imagination, reenact your steps with Holy Spirit as Helper. Picture Holy Spirit or Jesus watching you go throughout your day. Look through His eyes. Focus together on the last time you saw the object. What happened next? Where did you go? What did you do? Did you answer the phone? Did you go to the kitchen to get something to eat? Did a family member call you to a different room? Allow thoughts, pictures, ideas, and impressions to come to you from the Revealer of Mysteries. With the help of divine recall, retrace your steps and find your lost thing.

6
SENSITIVITY TRAINING

Did you ever play the game "Hot or Cold"? In this children's game, one person hides an object and the other hunts for it. As the hunter moves closer to the object, the hider voices clues. The nearer the hunter gets to the object, the more intense the clues: warmer, hot, hotter, burning, scorching.... The increasing heat and intensity of the clues tell the hunter they are getting closer to finding the object. If the hunter turns the wrong direction, the clues move in the opposite direction as well: cool, cold, freezing, icy....

The game reminds me of how the children of Israel were led through the desert.

> Nehemiah 9:12
> By day you led them with a pillar of cloud, and by night with a pillar of fire to give them light on the way they were to take.

Though it's not a perfect metaphor for the subject, we see this historical account of God leading His children with a cloud of cool by day and a fire of illumination by night. God led them by signs that we picture today as "hot" and "cold." Likewise, in the New Testament, the disciples were able to recognize Jesus by how their hearts burned within them. The sensation of fire in their hearts provided a witness from Holy Spirit as to the identity of their traveling companion and what He was saying. Let's look at this passage.

> Luke 24:32
> They said to each other, "Didn't our hearts burn within us while he was speaking with us on the road, while he was explaining the scriptures to us?"

The sensing of hot and cold is one of the forms of spiritual intelligence often connected to the gift of discerning of spirits. Training your sense of temperature through spiritual discernment can be fun, but it's not a game nor is it childish. The writer of Hebrews describes training your senses as a sign of maturity that comes through practice.

> Hebrews 5:14
> But solid food is for the mature, who because of practice have their senses trained to discern good and evil.

Many people fail to train their senses because they think that their senses are evil or inappropriately sensual. After all, most believers have heard the phrase, "You can't trust your feelings." Right? Not necessarily. Senses in your old nature tended towards sensuality, but senses in the original and new creation tend towards sensitivity.

You can see this principle in the contrast of the old and new nature in Paul's writing to the Ephesians.

> Ephesians 4:19
> Having lost all sensitivity, they have given themselves over to sensuality so as to indulge in every kind of impurity, and they are full of greed.

From the description in this verse, we can identify the original state of our senses: sensitivity. But when human beings do not acknowledge or follow God, sensitive people give their own senses over to what? Sensuality. You can regain and even upgrade your sensitivity by offering your senses to God as instruments of righteousness.

Through offering the members of your body to God, you can then use your body senses like a "metal detector" for finding lost objects. A metal detector transmits an electromagnetic field from the search coil into the ground. Any metal objects within that field will become energized and retransmit an electromagnetic field of its own. That's what triggers the beep or signal of a metal detector. This earthly invention is a good picture of how our senses can work in finding lost items. You follow a feeling or sensation by how "hot" or "cold" it is.

That's what my friend Cathy from California experienced in finding her lost wedding ring. This story has a special place in my heart because I lost my first wedding ring saving a drowning kid in a wave pool. (The lifeguard was busy talking to some girls and didn't even see the child flailing.) My wife graciously replaced my first simple wedding band with an upgraded diamond studded version that I unfortunately lost a few years later while water skiing on the Ohio River. By the way, I've owned my third and current wedding band for over thirty years. We ordered it a half size too small so I could barely get it off if I tried. Still, I wish I had heard Cathy's finder's story back then. Notice how Cathy used her senses to find her lost treasure.

> *We were at Lake Pyramid walking on the beach when I suddenly realized my wedding ring was gone. I was so panicked, but I calmed myself enough to pray and ask the Lord where to start looking. I waded back into the water until it seemed like the right place. I reached down, digging into the sand, and RIGHT THERE was my wedding ring! It was miraculous!*

See how Cathy waded out to what "seemed like the right place"? She was using her natural senses like a spiritual metal detector energized by Holy Spirit. This isn't the only time that Cathy followed her senses to find lost treasure. I love her finder's story of rescuing a young family member from a potentially dangerous situation.

> *We were living in the San Fernando Valley in Los Angeles. I had a phone call from our five-year-old niece who said she was at a motel with another family member. It was not a safe situation, and she definitely sounded afraid.*
> *The little girl was asking me to come get her when suddenly an adult interrupted and hung up the phone. I had no idea where the motel was, but I remembered hearing a lot of traffic noise. I felt like the Lord spoke, "Ventura Boulevard." So, I got in the car and drove, asking angels to guide me. There are many hotels, motels, and businesses on this huge street! I drove several miles right to the motel, found the frightened five-year-old, and took her home with me.*

In this incident, Cathy used her natural sense of hearing to identify the traffic in the background, so she knew it was a busy street. Then, she "felt like" the Lord gave her a general direction through the street name. This was not as much hearing as it was a spiritual nudge or sensation from Holy Spirit. She stayed in connection with Holy Spirit, watching and feeling her way along while asking for the intervention of angels and as a result drove straight to the location to find the troubled child.

ACTIVATE Sensitivity

1. CONNECT WITH FATHER. Connect with Father and His heart for lost things. Remember to not lean on your own understanding but seek direction from the Father by the Holy Spirit. (Proverbs 3:5-6) Engaging your logic and reasoning right now may make your spiritual sensitivity through your senses less effective. Trust in the Lord and let Him direct your steps.

2. OFFER ALL YOUR SENSES TO GOD. Your senses are instruments of good and righteousness; offer them to God as such. (Romans 6:13) Perhaps you will want to say a simple prayer: "I am totally yours God. Give me a sensitivity within my body to that which is lost."

3. USE YOUR SENSES. Picture the item you are looking for and walk around your house, following the sensations in your body by the leading of Holy Spirit. God isn't limited to only move through the senses of hot and cold. Pay attention to other sensations, for example heaviness, a tingle, a feeling of electricity, an inner impulse, or a tug deep in the pit of your stomach or heart.

4. FOLLOW THE SENSATIONS. Follow those increasing or diminishing sensations to find your lost item. Upon

finding that lost item, remember to rejoice in the Lord and give Him thanks.

7
FINDING WITH HEARING

IN THE LAST FEW YEARS, I've heard many preachers say the clever phrase: "The kingdom of God is voice-activated." I agree, but recently while watching my two-year-old granddaughter, I was reminded that the key to voice activation is voice recognition. My granddaughter loves to test the voice-activated technology in my home. We own a device that uses the Amazon Alexa voice-activated service. My granddaughter loves to speak to Alexa and ask "her" to play various songs, but the problem is Alexa doesn't always recognize what she is saying—frankly, there are times when none of us do. The point is the device must be trained to recognize the voice of the speaker in order to complete the command. This serves as a great metaphor. Voice activation requires voice recognition. Recognizing the voice of Jesus is the key to responding. We see this principle in scripture as Jesus said, "My sheep listen to my voice; I know them, and they follow me." (John 10:27)

The key to following the voice of Jesus is recognizing His voice.

> John 10:5
> But they will never follow a stranger; in fact, they will run away from him because they do not recognize a stranger's voice.

Voice-activation in the Kingdom depends upon your voice-recognition skills. Do you believe you can hear the voice of God? Do you recognize the many ways that He speaks? I love how in the first writings of Samuel, the prophet shares a story from his own childhood about how he first heard the audible voice of the Lord. An audible voice called the boy's name at night, but Samuel thought it was the voice of his priest. God persistently called him by name, but each time he ran to what he thought was the voice of his priest. Many people mistake the supernatural for something more explainable. The third time this happened, the mentor priest, Eli, finally recognized that it was God speaking to Samuel and taught the boy how to respond.

> 1 Samuel 3:9
> So Eli told Samuel, "Go and lie down, and if he calls you, say, "Speak, Lord, for your servant is listening."

Voice-recognition was the simple key that opened the whole supernatural realm to Samuel's recognizing and responding to the voice of God. Now you're beginning to understand the statement "voice activation requires voice recognition." If you don't know it is the voice of God speaking to you, then you don't know that you should respond. As we said earlier, young Samuel thought the spiritual voice was a natural one. Many of us make the same mistake. From other Bible accounts, we can see that Samuel was not alone in mistaking God's voice for something more natural. Shortly before his death, Jesus prayed, "Father, glorify Your Name!" An audible voice answered from heaven saying, "I have glorified it and will glorify it again!" Look at the response of the crowd who heard the audible voice of God as told by his close friend John.

> John 12:29
> The crowd that was there and heard it said it had thundered; others said an angel had spoken to him.

Some of the crowd heard the audible voice of God but explained it away as thunder. Sometimes the supernatural dies of natural causes. We reason away the voice of God with logic and rationalizations. We think, "That was just me," or "I'm just hearing things." We explain away supernatural leadings with natural reasoning. The above passage also points out that others in the crowd thought the voice was an angel. This group credited the sound to a spiritual source but didn't link it to God. This is too often the human condition—no expectation of hearing the voice of God. The lack of voice recognition skills leads to no activation. If per chance we do hear, we so often reason away what is said as something other than the voice of God. Yet, it is the privilege of every son and daughter of God to hear and know the voice of the Father.

This too, is a faith issue. If you are His sheep, then you can hear and follow His voice. Drive that concept as a stake in the ground, marking your claim to direction and leading. God speaks to His children, and hearing is a key to finding. Look at the following familiar verse with me very carefully.

> Luke 11:9
> So I say to you: "Ask and it will be given to you; seek and you will find; knock and the door will be opened to you."

This principle is sequential. The sequence of finding begins with the responsibility of asking. Your voice activates His voice. Ask Him where your lost thing is then get quiet and still. Listen internally with the heart while being attentive with your physical ears as you wait for His response. When He speaks, follow each impression with the appropriate second step of seeking. As the third instruction in the sequence, knocking implies moving from a general seeking to something much more specific and targeted.

Watch how asking opened the way for Lisa to hear more clearly where to seek for a missing passport while on a trip to the Holy Land. Here is her finder's story:

FINDING LOST THINGS

> *It was a rainy day, so a couple of ladies on the tour had gone into a small shop to purchase an umbrella for the walking tour. It wasn't until we had already finished the walk and boarded the bus to Caesarea Philippi that one lady from our team realized she had left her passport wallet on the counter at the store. When she realized it was missing, the team of 26 people completely tore up the bus and moved everything, clearing out from under her seat and searching through all of hers and her husband's things. It was nowhere to be found. She began to panic.*
>
> *The tour guide made a phone call to the store so that store personnel were on the alert for it, but they said they hadn't seen it. The owner of the passport was a little concerned that with the amount of money that was in the wallet, someone might not come forward even if they found it. We began to pray.*
>
> *We arrived at our lunch spot, and everyone got off the bus but the three of us. The lady with the lost passport, her husband, and I stayed on the bus and searched with a fine-toothed comb. We had taken all the belongings out of the seat and out from under it; the missing passport wallet was still nowhere to be found. The three of us decided to go get something cold to drink and wait inside out of*

the rain while the bus driver ran back to the shop to look for it.

The woman was crying and said, "Lisa, I know you prayed. Did God tell you where the passport is?" At that moment I answered, "No. He didn't, but I didn't ask. I'm going to ask right now." With a loud voice in the restaurant I just said, "Lord, I know that you know where this passport is and I'm trusting you to tell me. Please, reveal it's whereabouts." I heard a very clear audible voice say, "It's on the bus. Go look under the seat." I spoke up in a loud voice, "The Lord said that it is on the bus under the seat." The husband and wife both reminded me that we had taken everything off that bus, and it was nowhere to be found. I said, "You told me to ask the Lord where it was, and this is what He said. So, you need to go look again."

Begrudgingly, the husband went out and asked the bus driver to unlock the door so he could look under the seat. Lo and behold, it was sitting right there in the middle of an open space surrounded by nothing. He came off the bus just scratching his head and saying, "No way. There is no way that we all missed it sitting right there in the open. How can this be?" So, I asked the Lord how we had missed it, and He said, "You didn't. I sent an angel to deliver it."

> *We were all praising and thanking God for His goodness, and I think that situation opened the hearts of this group to see that God still speaks to us. He cares about the things which concern us, and He is right there with us on this journey.*

Not everyone hears an audible voice like Lisa, but it happens more than you might think. The Lord also speaks to our hearts and through our thoughts. If nothing seems to be happening, begin to walk around your search area. You have asked, now begin to seek which is the second step in the finder's sequence of Luke 11. As you move about the search area, you are engaging an additional promise of divine direction spoken through the prophet Isaiah.

Isaiah 30:21
Whether you turn to the right or to the left,
your ears will hear a voice behind you, saying,
"This is the way; walk in it."

If you don't hear a voice out in front of you leading you, then start seeking and see if you can engage the one behind you. Kathy heard the voice behind her when looking for an essential part for her business. Here is her finder's story:

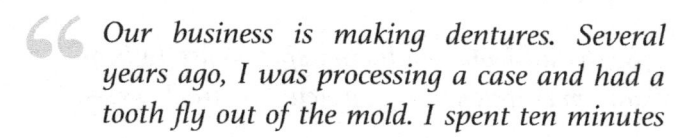

> *Our business is making dentures. Several years ago, I was processing a case and had a tooth fly out of the mold. I spent ten minutes*

> *looking all around the place where I thought it would be—under the table in front of me—with no results. Finally, I asked God where it was. I heard Him in my spirit say, "Look behind you." I obeyed the inner voice and found the tooth in a small crevasse under the counter directly behind me.*

Kathy could have looked all day where she thought it was, but the Lord's voice redirected her to the actual location. Kathy is not the only one with a finder's story about hearing the voice of God. Kate from the United Kingdom also heard the voice behind her. She had lost her passport and was leaving for France in less than two weeks. She shared this account with a friend:

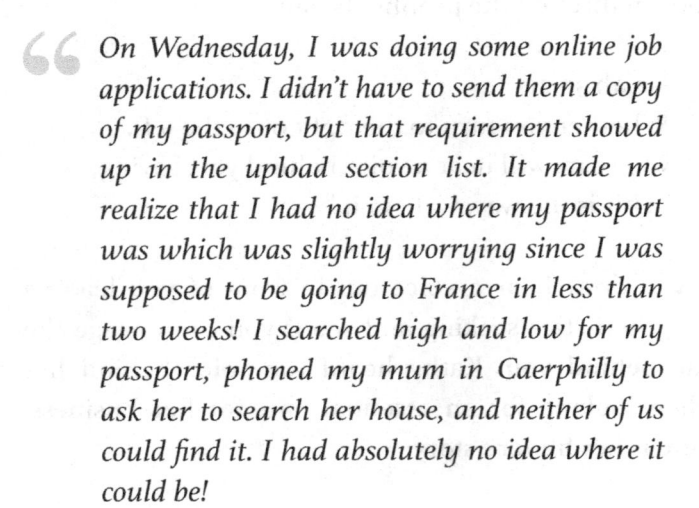

> *On Wednesday, I was doing some online job applications. I didn't have to send them a copy of my passport, but that requirement showed up in the upload section list. It made me realize that I had no idea where my passport was which was slightly worrying since I was supposed to be going to France in less than two weeks! I searched high and low for my passport, phoned my mum in Caerphilly to ask her to search her house, and neither of us could find it. I had absolutely no idea where it could be!*
>
> *So, today I phoned the passport office to book an appointment to get a new fast track one—*

something that I really couldn't afford to do. Anyway, I left work today feeling pretty stressed about the whole thing. As I was driving home, God spoke to me and said, "Pray about it." I started to pray and asked God to, "Please! Please, help me find it!"

I started to feel like there was no point. (I had been feeling pretty disconnected from God lately.) As that feeling emerged, straight away God said to me, "You aren't praying hard enough. Be bold!" So, I gave it a go and prayed some more. As I did, I remembered you were saying that if you fully believe that God is going to answer your prayers, he will! I started telling myself this and really believed that God was going to help me out. As I did this, I heard a voice as clear as if He was sitting in my car with me. The voice said, "Your passport is right behind you." When I pulled up outside my house, I got out of the car and pulled my seat forward. There it was! I can honestly say that I have never before had such a strong encounter with God. It feels absolutely incredible! I've been bouncing around the house all day.

Kate's story shows the importance of asking in faith. How you ask is as important as what you ask. The point was not to pray louder, but Kate did need to pray bolder and with expectancy of hearing. God honors faith. When Kate prayed, God began to answer in a progression of dialogue. He said, "Pray more boldly." As she prayed more earnestly, she was reminded of the necessity of believing when you ask. Do you see how her action of asking started a chain reaction of being led by God? It wasn't just about saying words; true prayer requires earnest faith. Then, as Kate followed the leading of Holy Spirit, she heard the voice behind that led to finding the passport.

Kate's progression of prayer and faith reminds me of a verse from the Book of James:

> James 5:16 NLT
> The earnest prayer of a righteous person has
> great power and produces wonderful results.

As her words took on an earnest faith, they began to produce something powerful. Asking is a key to receiving; seeking is the key to finding; and knocking is the specific direction of Holy Spirit. Finding is often a relational progression. Prayer is meant to be a conversation not a monologue. As you ask, listen; as you seek, listen. Hold fast to the promise of His voice guiding you before and after.

God's promise of direction reminds me of the response on an old GPS (Global Positioning System). If you take a wrong turn or go past your exit, the GPS voice says, "Recalculating, recalculating." In a similar way, even if you overlook where God is leading, He has a way to get you back on track. A voice behind you will say, "Over here. This is the way." Your voice in prayer and faith activates His voice of guidance for finding that which is lost.

Here is another principle that may prove helpful in your finding mission: The voice of the Lord does not always say something logical or reasonable to the natural mind. As in this story submitted by my friend Rob from Australia, sometimes you might find your lost thing in an unexpected or unusual place.

> *My family and I attended the local school fete[1] one evening to watch the fireworks. We took a blanket and sat and watched a fantastic fireworks display full of color and excitement. At the end, we packed up our things and headed to the car to drive home because it was far past our children's normal bedtime, and they were letting us know it. When we got to the car with arms full of sleepy, grumpy kids and picnic items, that dreaded sinking feeling of—NO WAY! I have lost the keys—hit me.*
>
> *I tore everything apart, turned every pocket inside out, and responded to a barrage of sleeping kids' comments. I figured I must have lost the keys somewhere...maybe where we were sitting? I retraced my steps while leaving my wife and kids at the car, all the while running scenarios through my head like, "Ok I live about 30 minutes' walk from here. Do I go now and get the spare key, or do I call a friend*

or what do I do?" I just started quietly at first saying, "Jesus, I need you; please help me to find these keys" over and over to myself. I got back to the area where we sat to watch the fireworks and looked everywhere but still could not find any keys.

I thought, "Maybe someone has picked them up and will return them to the school office." As I started walking back to my car, I remembered Bill Johnson once told a testimony about wanting something back. As I recalled this, I felt an emotion like an injustice rising in me. I started to declare quite loudly, "Lord, I need my keys to take my family home! You love them more than I ever could. Please, I want the keys back to get them out of the cold and home safely!"

As I was walking back to the car still declaring out loud, I heard that still small voice of the Lord say, "Look near that tree." It was just a normal looking tree in a row of about 10 trees —nothing special or unusual about it. But as I walked towards it, at the base of the tree there were my keys. The odd thing was, I did not walk near this tree or close enough to it to be able to drop keys at the base of it underneath the outstretched branches. Someone must have thrown them there, or it was an absolute miracle. But there they were. I picked them up and told my family about how God found the keys, and we all prayed and thanked God on the way home.

Whether you hear an audible voice, a heart voice, or a voice behind you, expect to hear the voice of the Lord. He still speaks to us today, tangibly and practically, especially concerning that which is lost.

ACTIVATE Hearing

1. MAKE A HEARING DECLARATION. Declare from a heart position, "I am your child. I can hear and follow the voice of My Father. Speak Lord, your servant is listening."

2. LISTEN WITH YOUR HEART. Stay still for a moment and listen with your heart, listen with your physical ears, and listen for God's voice in your thoughts. Write down any impressions, thoughts, or words the Lord speaks to you and then act on them.

3. KEEP LISTENING. While you are seeking, keep listening to the voice of the Lord. If you get off track in your search, trust that His voice will redirect you and get you back on course for finding your missing item.

8
FINDING WITH SEEING

IT'S AN ALL-TOO-COMMON OCCURRENCE. I'm looking for a tool to fix that loose screw on the switch plate. "Honey!" I call, "Have you seen my screwdriver?"

She calls back, "I think I saw it in the other room on the counter." I go to that room and search the entire counter.

"No!" I call back, "It's not there."

Then she walks down the stairs, enters the room, picks up the screwdriver from the counter right in front of me, and hands it to me with that "what would you do without me" smile. It's embarrassing. Why couldn't I see the item even with clear directions? It was right in front of me, but I couldn't see it.

Psychologists tell us that seeing is a motivated perception. In other words, what we choose to see is not always an accurate representation of what truly is.

Seeing is a function of the eyes gathering information and the brain interpreting what it determines to be essential data. Seeing is simply one perception of a greater reality. The problem is that our perceptions of seeing are often biased, selective, and shapeable. We see what we think we will see. For instance, I looked on the counter for the screwdriver, but I didn't expect to see it; therefore, my brain somehow filtered out that visual information as unnecessary. My eyes received the information, but my brain filtered it out because a person only sees what they believe they will see. I saw what I expected to see.

This process happens in what is called your Reticular Activating System or RAS. RAS is a bundle of nerves at your brainstem that filters out unnecessary information so that the important stuff gets through. The RAS is the reason you buy a new car that you think is unique and then begin to see it everywhere. Your RAS takes what you focus on and creates a filter for it. It then sifts through all the data and presents back to you only the pieces that it determines are important to you. Without the RAS, you would be overloaded with visual information and not able to focus. Your Reticular Activating System seeks information that validates your beliefs. This complex brain function filters the outside world through the parameters that you give it, and your beliefs are one of the things that shape those parameters. Perhaps this explains how we can have "eyes to see, but not see." (Ezekiel 12:2)

When it comes to finding a lost thing, you must reboot your brain's search parameters. If you think you have looked everywhere, then you won't see it anywhere, even if it is sitting right in front of you. Your RAS parameters will block or filter out your ability to see reality clearly.

So how do you reset those brain filters? Start by truly believing that you will see and find your missing item. I know. That sounds too simple, but it is a good start. Set the position of your heart and mind by speaking out a declaration: "I'm sure I will find this. I will see it soon. Thank you, Father, that You have given me eyes that see." This sends your brain the signal that allows you to see what otherwise might be filtered out by the RAS as unnecessary data.

Now, as best as you know how, shut out the history of where you have already looked. Reboot your search engine as if you are searching for the first time. Start fresh in your spirit like one who has not yet looked. Dismiss the idea that your item can't possibly be here or there because you have already looked here and there. Displace that idea with something like, "I know it is here somewhere."

This type of search reminds me of the parable of the lost coin.

> Luke 15:8
> Or suppose a woman has ten silver coins and loses one. Won't she light a lamp and sweep the

> entire house and search carefully until she finds it?"

The woman who lost the coin kept lighting the way, sweeping the house, and searching carefully. She didn't say, "Oh, I already looked there so it can't be there." No. She believed it was in her house, so she searched with an expectancy of finding. This faith position and declaration helps set your RAS filters to seeing and finding what is lost.

In addition to your natural vision, you can search with internal vision. Allow an image or picture to form in your imagination. Imagination is the most powerful "nation" in the world. God has gifted you with imagination; learn to use it for Him. This is part of the outpouring of the Spirit on all flesh that was promised through the Prophet Joel.

> Joel 2:28
> And afterward, I will pour out my Spirit on all people. Your sons and daughters will prophesy, your old men will dream dreams, your young men will see visions.

Visions are part of the generous provision of God in the outpouring of Holy Spirit on all people. Though seeing a vision of pictorial sequences playing out like a movie in front of you can be a bit mystical, a vision can also be as simple as a snapshot picture or an idea that suddenly pops into your head. That's what happened to me when a friend had lost her cell phone. Here is one of my simple finder's stories:

> *Our children's pastor, Amanda, lost her iPhone® and had searched everywhere. She mentioned it to me, and I immediately and involuntarily saw a snapshot of her setting the phone on a round table in the youth room upstairs. The picture wasn't totally logical because our church campus is huge; the children's department is mostly downstairs, and the youth room is upstairs on the other side of the building. I pressed past the unlikely sense of my impression and shared it anyway.*
>
> *"Hey," I asked, "Did you go up to the youth room for anything?"*
>
> *"Yes," she answered a bit surprised, "I borrowed some supplies."*
>
> *Her answer gave me the confidence to continue, "Check on the round table by the stage in the youth room." She went upstairs, walked to that exact location, and found her phone.*
>
> *The image came to me as a brief passing snapshot of divine revelation.*

A vision or sudden involuntary snapshot image is often how God will reveal the location of a lost item.

Nadine from South Africa experienced this with her lost cell phone.

> *I was looking for my cellphone everywhere. Eventually, I asked Holy Spirit to show me where it was. Then, Holy Spirit showed me a picture. In the picture I saw the floor underneath my car seat; and when I looked under my car seat, it was lying there on the floor. Yeah! So cool when you can just ask Holy Spirit to help you.*

Another form of vision is when information appears as a symbol or metaphor that needs to be interpreted. Spiritual intelligence often comes in symbolic form. Be open to that possibility. In other words, you might receive an involuntary picture of a hammer. That doesn't necessarily mean that your missing item is in the toolbox next to your hammer; the hammer might represent your workplace, meaning you left the item on your desk at work. God loves to speak through parables, metaphors, and symbols. A picture is worth a thousand words, but pictures also can require interpretation.

Dreams are another powerful form of seeing in the Spirit. God can guide you to your lost item through seeing its location in a literal or symbolic dream. Some people have reported success in searching for lost things by focusing on the Lord and His grace in finding lost things just before slipping off to sleep. This is not a matter of worrying or fretting about the lost item before you go to bed but setting your heart on the nature of God as a finder while remembering what it is you are looking for. Some are able to develop this skill intentionally while other finders have shared that this mainly happens to them involuntarily. If your day eyes have failed to produce results, then assign the night crew of dreams to your search. Whether searching with your natural eyes or prompted by one of these forms of spiritual vision or dreams, seeing is a finder's tool that can be sharpened and guided by Holy Spirit.

ACTIVATE Seeing

1. RESET YOUR EXPECTATION. When searching with your natural eyes, make sure you reset your RAS with a fresh expectation of seeing and finding what you are looking for. Remember the power of your declarations and say something like "I know it is here somewhere. Thank you, Lord, for giving me eyes to see it."

2. TRY LOOKING WITH YOUR SPIRITUAL EYES. Pray a simple prayer of dedication: "Thank you, Father, for pouring your Spirit out on all people so that we can see dreams and visions. Open the eyes of my heart Lord to see this lost thing. (Ephesians 1:18-19) Close your natural eyes and pay attention to any images or impressions that come to your imagination.

3. TRY SEARCHING IN THE DREAM REALM. Meditate on the nature of God as a finder and think about your lost item just before slipping off to sleep. Keep a note pad or recording device near your bed to capture information you receive while dreaming.

9
FINDING WITH KNOWING

IN MY TWENTIES AND THIRTIES, I had an amazing spiritual mentor named Cleddie Keith. I served him as a youth pastor and worship leader for twelve years. Pastor Cleddie would always seem to know things by the power of the Holy Spirit. For example, he would announce that so-and-so is going to call today. Then, the phone would ring, and it would be that person. These kinds of precognitive things were common occurrences with him. Once when the two of us were driving to a conference in another city, I noticed that Pastor Cleddie began to veer off the mapped route.

I asked, "Where are we going?" He answered very matter of factly that we were going to see brother so-and-so. I thought that was a strange answer because we had limited time to get to the conference and that person lived in the opposite direction and in a different city than where we were heading.

I reminded him, "But, he doesn't live in this city."

"I know," Cleddie answered, "but we are going to see him." He made several turns in a city neither of us knew well and then pulled the car to a sudden stop at the entrance of a Walmart.

At that very moment, that pastor came walking out of the Walmart store right up to our car scratching his head and asking, "Why, Cleddie, what are you doing here?"

Such was the adventurous life of working with Pastor Cleddie. Oftentimes, when he manifested these sudden perceptions of unexplainable information, I asked, "How did you know that?"

He answered, "I just knew it in my 'knower.'" I think his answer is one of the best descriptions of the finder's skill we are talking about in this chapter—knowing with your knower.

Knowing in your heart or the grace of precognition is a form of a revelation gift of Holy Spirit. Revelation can be defined as "a surprising and previously unknown fact, especially one that is made known in a dramatic way" or "the divine or supernatural disclosure to humans of something relating to human existence or the world."[1]

The term "sudden revelation" reminds me of the Bible account of when Jesus asked his disciples the question, "Who do you say that I am?" Most of the disciples shared the typical answers of their day, but Peter blurted out, "You are the Christ, the Son of the Living

God." Jesus identified the source of Peter's sudden revelation by saying, "Blessed are you, Simon son of Jonah, for this was not revealed to you by flesh and blood, but by my Father in heaven." (Matthew 16:16-18) Peter's perception was not based on human reasoning or mere observation but upon a sudden revelation of Holy Spirit. He knew it in his knower.

Jesus often manifested sudden perceptions of people's thoughts, motives, and future actions. (See Matthew 9:4, 22:18, Mark 5:30, Luke 9:47, John 6:15, 6:64, 13:1, 16:19, 18:4) Paul the apostle also had significant supernatural encounters with sudden knowing. (Acts 23:6, 27:10) Knowing, perceiving, and precognition by the power of Holy Spirit are helpful finder's tools. It may seem strange to experience something as completely lost one moment and then have sudden unexplainable knowledge of where that item is located the next, but it happens quite often.

This was the case for the Flanagan family in South Africa. One moment they were tearing apart the house looking for a lost toy, and the next moment there was a sudden revelation of its location. Here is their finder's story:

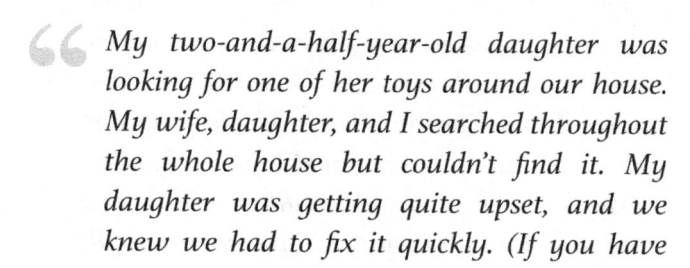

> *My two-and-a-half-year-old daughter was looking for one of her toys around our house. My wife, daughter, and I searched throughout the whole house but couldn't find it. My daughter was getting quite upset, and we knew we had to fix it quickly. (If you have*

> *kids, you'll know what I mean!) I then said, "Let's stop and pray and ask Jesus to show us where it is." Straight away after that prayer, my daughter quickly went to one of our couches and lifted up a pillow. The toy was right there! I'm not sure how she heard from God, but it was clear that she got some type of download. My daughter was ecstatic, and Jesus got a big, "Hallelujah!"*

Some might attribute this to a sudden remembering (divine recall which we talked about earlier) and certainly that could be the case, but moving from not-knowing to sudden knowing is that "lightbulb moment" of revelation that provides welcome answers in times of stressful loss. Here is another brief story of a lost toy where the mother, Rhea, was the one with the sudden revelation. In this case, there is no way she could have known where the item was apart from the revelation of Holy Spirit. Here is her finder's story:

> *When my son, Josiah, was 6, he lost his little brother's favorite toy—a tiny Chewbacca figurine from the Star Wars series. We got home from an event, and it was late and dark. Josiah dropped it somewhere and was crying with remorse because he knew the toy was special to his brother. He began to pray and cry out to God. As he prayed, I suddenly knew exactly where to look. I walked outside and found the tiny brown toy in the dark in a pile*

> *of wet brown leaves in the very first place I looked. Now, anytime something goes missing, the boys' first response is to pray.*

How did Rhea know where the lost toy was when she didn't see it dropped? She just "knew it in her knower." Imagine what would have been the potential difficulty of trying to find a tiny brown figure at night in wet brown leaves! That little brown toy was practically camouflaged. Mom's sudden revelatory perception was a supernatural tool called a word of knowledge. This spiritual gift is identified among the nine manifestation gifts Paul unveiled in his letter to the Corinthian church. (1 Corinthians 12:8-11) The word of knowledge gift often manifests as a sudden thought, impression, picture, or compulsion to act. That's what happened in Nick's story when the young military recruit lost an important chip in his government-issued ID card.

> *I am a part of the United States Army. When you join, they issue you a CAC (Common Access Card) which has your photo ID, your Department of Defense ID number, and other info hosted on a chip that computers will recognize when you log in. A few months ago, as I was trying to log in to my work computer, I removed the card to discover that the chip was missing. Imagine that the chip of your credit card or debit card suddenly disappeared —that is what happened to me. I told my*

> *supervisor who informed me that I needed to try my hardest to find the chip because it posed a potential security risk. If someone with malicious intent found the chip, they could use it to gain access to information they shouldn't have.*
>
> *As I stared at my chip-less card, feeling puzzled, the word "hallway" came to mind. I almost dismissed it thinking, "What are the odds?" But I chose to investigate. Not five paces from the door to my office section was the computer chip laying on the ground in the hallway. When that happened, I realized that the Lord had given me a word of knowledge without my having prayed for one. It was pretty exciting to have this happen.*

As I have already mentioned, this is how words of knowledge often manifest. An image, idea, or impression just "pops" into your head. Sometimes the impression passes as quickly as it comes, so it is important to catch it quickly and pay attention. Words of knowledge often come as a sudden revelation of just knowing in your knower. For Nadine from South Africa, her missing item's whereabouts came in the form of a sudden thought. Here is her finder's story:

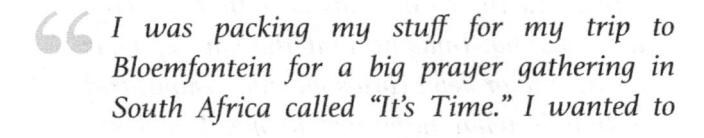

> *I was packing my stuff for my trip to Bloemfontein for a big prayer gathering in South Africa called "It's Time." I wanted to*

charge my power bank and was looking everywhere for it. I had last seen it on the coffee table, but it was not there. I asked my mom if she saw it, and she said, "Yes, the power bank is on the coffee table." So, I looked again, and it was not there.

I looked everywhere and could not find it. I really needed my power bank because I would not be able to charge my cellphone on the bus, and the distance from my home to Bloemfontein was 11 hours. After a while, I was really tired of looking for it, and I prayed asking God where the power bank was. My sister's name "Tanya" popped into my head. I sent a message to my sister to ask her if she knew where the power bank was. She said, "Yes. Sorry." She was at our house earlier that day, and her phone died, so she used my power bank to charge her phone and had taken it with her to her house. I told her I was looking for it everywhere, and Holy Spirit told me that she had it. This was cool. It was a time where I was learning to hear God's voice.

Knowing or perceiving is a common way to receive information from Holy Spirit. Many people overlook these types of impressions because the information is not necessarily passing through their physical senses. In other words, the impressions are not appearing as dreams, visions, hearing a voice, or having a strong feeling. The perception of knowing or precognition most often arrives as an impression in the heart like an inner conviction. The perceptions are so internal that we often don't recognize them as something supernatural.

To me, these moments of perceiving feel like something I already knew rather than a divine download from heaven. Yet, upon a moment's reflection, I'm totally aware that I had no previous knowledge of the thing revealed. If you have experienced this, then you probably know what I'm talking about. If you've never experienced a moment of sudden revelation like this, then you may be asking, "How do I access this divine ability to know in my knower or perceive by a word of knowledge?"

Perception is a prophetic grace that can be developed through knowledge, grace, and practice. Remember that God's Holy Spirit has been poured out on all people so that everyone can have prophetic perceptions. Our former state was dull and darkened as shared in the writings of the prophets and declared by Apostle Paul.

> Acts 28:26-27
> Go to this people and say, "You will be ever hearing but never understanding; you will be ever seeing but never perceiving." For this people's heart has become calloused; they hardly hear with their ears, and they have closed their eyes. Otherwise they might see

> with their eyes, hear with their ears,
> understand with their hearts and turn, and I
> would heal them.

It was a calloused heart that kept us from perceiving and understanding, but when we turn to God, He heals us and replaces our heart of stone with a tender impressionable heart. Turning your heart to the Lord in this way opens the door to knowing, perceiving, and understanding by the power of Holy Spirit.

In addition to perceiving, we have the gifts of the Spirit. As I shared earlier, word of knowledge is a gift of the Spirit spoken of in 1 Corinthians 12:8. Though that same chapter makes it clear that each of us have differing gifts assigned to us as God chooses, the last verse of the chapter tells us to "earnestly desire greater gifts." (1 Corinthians 12:31) God wouldn't encourage us to desire something from Him that He is not willing to give to us. This verse is God granting us permission and faith to seek new and greater gifts of the Spirit such as word of knowledge. Just ask God for the gift, remembering that He is a generous giver.

Knowing and perceiving by the power of Holy Spirit are great finder's tools. The more aware you are of this form of divine communication, the more accurate and helpful you can be in seeking and saving that which is lost.

ACTIVATE Knowing

1. Ask for words of knowledge. Start with the simple practice we have mentioned before of not leaning on your own understanding but acknowledging God in all your ways. (Proverbs 3:5-6) Make a simple declaration of something like "Holy Spirit, you know where my missing thing is. I ask for the gift of word of knowledge and for You to heighten my perceptions by opening my ability to know and perceive."

2. Pay attention. Take notice of any impression, conviction, or idea that comes to you. You may want to write down the details so you don't forget anything.

3. Act quickly and confidently. Act on what is revealed with an expectancy to find your missing item. Be sure to thank the Lord for His goodness in revealing this hidden knowledge by the grace and power of Holy Spirit.

10

SIGNS AND WONDERS

LOGIC AND RATIONAL THINKING can only take you so far when accessing spiritual intel about your missing item. Most supernatural breakthroughs come from following the intuitive heart rather than the natural intellect. In searching for lost things, we so often lean on our own understanding and then wonder why we come up short. For many years, I wondered at the ways of God. "God," I asked, "why are your ways so illogical? They just don't make sense." Years later, I received the answer. While God's ways may seem to defy logic, they actually transcend it with higher wisdom and knowledge. Though the concept came as a fresh understanding to me, it's certainly not a new idea. The prophet Isaiah declared this truth over 2,700 years ago.

> Isaiah 55:9
> As the heavens are higher than the earth, so are my ways higher than your ways and my thoughts than your thoughts.

God's ways and reasons are infinitely higher than ours. One reason we miss God's ways of transcendent wisdom is because they often seem foolish or illogical to the natural mind. The New Testament scripture, however, declares that the foolishness of God is wiser than human wisdom. (1 Corinthians 1:25) One implication of this truth is that God's ways can look foolish or crazy to the rational mind. Understanding this is a key to following God's wisdom. For this reason, when searching for your lost item, it may be foolish for you to not consider a more "out-of-the-box" idea or search method.

Where do we start in recognizing God's higher wisdom that may look like earthly foolishness? How do we access transcendent information? It starts with putting away fear. In your search for lost things, do not be afraid to look or sound foolish. As I have implied before, God's instructions don't always seem logical.

Remember the Bible story where Peter had fished all night and caught nothing? (Luke 5:5 and John 21:3) We might even say that the fish were "missing." Bible historians tell us that Simon Peter was likely born to a family of experienced fishermen. What the Lord told Peter to do sounded totally crazy in an earthly paradigm, "Throw your net on the other side." Simon Peter could easily have responded, "Listen, Lord, You know preaching and spiritual stuff, but I know fishing. It just doesn't work that way." But Peter, in this case, didn't lean on his own years of experience and natural understanding; he chose to listen and obey the transcendent wisdom. Following one seemingly foolish command netted Simon Peter one of the greatest catches of fish in his entire life. He found his missing catch of fish by following the wisdom of transcendent thinking.

We have another example of God's foolish-looking ways of finding lost things documented in 2 Kings chapter six. One of the young prophetic students had lost an axe head in the river while cutting down a tree. He was in a panic because the axe head was borrowed, and he apparently like many poor students had no way to purchase a new one. Of course, there also weren't any hardware stores nearby. He ran to the prophet for counsel. Observe with me the strange finding method used by this great spiritual leader.

> 2 Kings 6:5-7
> But as one of them was cutting down a tree, the iron axe head fell into the water. "Oh no, my lord!" he cried out. "It was borrowed!" The man of God asked, "Where did it fall?" When he showed him the place, Elisha cut a stick and threw it there, and made the iron float. "Lift it out," he said. Then the man reached out his hand and took it.

Let's recap this story in a fun way.

"Ok, so you lost something in the water?"

"Yes."

"And you have tried everything you know to find it?"

"Yes."

"Well, have you tried cutting a stick and throwing it in the water?"

"What? That doesn't make sense. That can't work."

Oh, but it did. When we are willing to consider seemingly illogical promptings of Holy Spirit, signs and wonders become powerful tools within our search engine. By suspending logic, transcendent thinking moves us toward higher wisdom and knowledge.

I love Jen's finder's story that occurred while moving from Southern to Northern California. Her act of obedient shopping enabled her to find and restore two lost sets of earrings.

> *About 9 years ago, when I lived in LA, I had two pair of identical owl face earrings, except that one pair was made of silver and the other pair copper. When I moved to Humboldt in Northern California, somehow in the move only one earring of each set made it to our new home. I had one mismatched set left, so they sat in my jewelry box for several years collecting dust until about a year and a half ago.*
>
> *God sometimes speaks to me in that thin fleeting moment between asleep and awake, and in those moments, His voice sounds like a*

person is there talking in the room. One morning in a season when I had been praying for wisdom, I dreamed an owl flew over my house. In my half-awake state I heard the words "Wisdom is only sleeping, like stored treasure." I should say that to me owls represent wisdom, so I remembered those earrings and decided to wear the unmatched set that day.

My small town of Arcata has a donation store called Scrap that specializes in all things incomplete for cheap. There you can find half balls of yarn, open stationery sets, wine corks for crafts, single markers—you name it. I knew I had been needing to go there to get more thread for the God's Eye ornaments I was making. I was planning on going the next day because I had a ton to do that day, but I couldn't shake the feeling that for some reason Holy Spirit really wanted me to go that particular day. So, I went.

While there to get thread, I noticed they were having a jewelry sale for one day only. In this sale, you buy a big random bag for $5 and whatever is in it could be really cool, could be junk, or could be a mix—you just don't know until after you pay. I wasn't going to buy a bag until I remembered the words from my half-awake vision, "sleeping like stored treasure." With that memory in mind, I

> *purchased the random bag and somehow, there in that bag, were the exact same owl face earrings identical to the mismatched ones I was wearing, one silver and one copper. I now have two perfectly matched pair again.*

Wow! God's voice has creative power, and responding to His voice releases things otherwise considered impossible. Everything about Jen's story sounds illogical and unreasonable, but this kind of transcendent thinking is often a key to supernatural finding. You must be willing to get "out of your mind." If you follow God's instructions, you will likely be accused of being crazy, fanatical, or deluded, but I try to take those types of comments as a compliment and affirmation that I'm truly letting God lead. Paul said it this way, "If we are 'out of our mind,' as some say, it is for God; if we are in our right mind, it is for you."(2 Corinthians 5:13) The phrase "out of our mind" in the Greek language means "to throw out of position, to displace, to throw into wonderment."

This phrase "out of your mind" reminds me of a quote Albert Einstein was reported to have said: "You cannot solve a problem with the same mindset that created it." Though the quote lacks clear documentation, the idea is consistent with many of the genius' other teachings. Einstein was saying that getting out of your current way of thinking is the key to solving your problem. The challenge is how do we get "out of our minds"?

One way is to embrace the power and blessing of God's transcendent thinking. There is a reason God gives us crazy instructions at times. He invites us into something totally illogical in the natural realm so that we can practice faith and walking in the Spirit realm to access a higher way of thinking. Revelation is a higher form of truth than fact. It is when we are not thinking on a transcendent level that we are most likely to not understand. In these moments, we must simply choose to trust and obey. The act of crazy faith and obedience offers you the opportunity to get outside of your current way of thinking and embrace transcendent truth. Not only will you often find your lost item and have an unbelievable testimony like Jen's, but you also are exposed to a higher standard of wisdom which then expands your faith for taking hold of wisdom in other areas. That's what we call a "win-win."

Sometimes the sign and wonder of transcendent ways is demonstrated in how the item is found. Celeste shares a story from her childhood of finding a lost camera in a river.

> *When I was a kid, my brother and I went with my dad early one morning to get prawns from the river. My mom gave me our camera to take some snaps as we were on holiday. Whilst walking in the river up to my knees in the semi-darkness, I suddenly realized I had lost the camera. It must have fallen out of my*

> *pocket, and the camera had all of our precious holiday snaps on it.*
>
> *I was so desperate; I just stood still and prayed to the Lord for help. When you search for prawns, you use a pump that makes the water murky. In addition to the murky water, we had been walking in the river for ages. Still, while I was praying, I looked down, and it was like the water just cleared in front of me. There, in the water at my feet was the camera! I picked it up, shook out the water, and carried on taking photos.*
>
> *The camera still worked, and the only evidence it had been in the water was a couple of water spots that showed up on the photos when the film was later developed. That camera worked for many years until we retired it because of new technology.*

Celeste could have lost that camera anywhere along the river hike. The river was muddied from the pump they were using. How could the water just suddenly clear and the lost camera appear at her feet? How could the camera still work? It doesn't make sense, but it doesn't matter that it doesn't make sense. God's ways are transcendent and believing someone else's testimony can be a key to starting your own journey towards finding lost items using signs and wonders.

. . .

ACTIVATE Signs and Wonders

1. LET GO OF THE RATIONAL. To the best of your ability, let go of every rational thought concerning your lost item. You have probably already looked everywhere and done everything you needed to do, so why not just let go of what is rational and logical. Surrender your rational mind to the transcendent thinking of God, "Father, I release what seems rational and reasonable to my limited understanding. I trust in you."

2. INVITE THE LORD. Offer a simple prayer that might go something like this, "God, let's do something crazy together. Show me the wisdom of God that looks totally foolish to men." Choose to get "out of your mind" through an act of surrender and simple trust.

3. ACT ON WHAT THE LORD TELLS YOU. From a place of child-like confidence, act on what the Lord tells you. Go search for your item according to your transcendent instructions. Remember, the more irrational the action the better for your new way of thinking. Nothing is too small, too simple, or too ludicrous. Childlike faith and obedience are the goal, and even if you miss it, the exercise will bear fruit in other areas.

4. BE THANKFUL. If you find your item, thank the Lord and embrace a new level of thinking. If you haven't found it yet, then thank the Lord for the experiment and embrace one of the other finding methods in this book.

11
ANGELS ON ASSIGNMENT

WOULDN'T IT BE GREAT to have your own personal search and rescue team? What if an amazing professional team of seekers is currently available to you right now? I'm talking about angels. I know many people are not comfortable talking about angels, but the scripture is certainly not hesitant to talk about them. Angels are mentioned 273 times in the Bible. I refer to them as a search and rescue team because they are described as helpers in the Book of Hebrews.

> Hebrews 1:14
> Are not all angels ministering spirits sent to
> serve those who will inherit salvation?

Here in Hebrews, we see the angels' assignment to serve those who will inherit salvation. God has ordained a partnership between man and angels. One of the ways angels serve is in search and rescue missions. Here are two of the many Bible stories that demonstrate their ability to search and rescue. The context for the first story is that the apostle Peter has been put into prison unjustly and was likely to receive a death sentence. Let's jump into the heart of this search and rescue:

> Acts 12:7-11
> Suddenly an angel of the LORD appeared, and a light shone in the cell. He struck Peter on the side and woke him up. "Quick, get up!" he said, and chains fell off Peter's wrists. Then the angel said to him, "Put on your clothes and sandals." And Peter did so. "Wrap your cloak around you and follow me," the angel told him. Peter followed him out of the prison, but he had no idea that what the angel was doing was really happening; he thought he was seeing a vision. They passed the first and second guards and came to the iron gate leading to the city. It opened for them by itself, and they went through it. When they had walked the length of one street, suddenly the angel left him. Then Peter came to himself and said, "Now I know without a doubt that the Lord has sent his angel and rescued me from Herod's clutches and from everything the Jewish people were hoping would happen."

This was not the only angelic jailbreak of this heavenly search and rescue team. A number of apostles were set free by a helper angel who also gave them an assignment.

> Acts 5:18-20
> They arrested the apostles and put them in the public jail. But during the night an angel of the LORD opened the doors of the jail and brought them out. "Go, stand in the temple courts," he said, "and tell the people all about this new life."

Finding and rescuing people is not the only assignment of the angels. We also see angels supplying food to Elijah (1 Kings 19:5-7) and comfort to Jesus after His forty-day fast. (Luke 4:11, Mark 1:13) We see angels throughout the Bible helping and serving people in various ways. How do we enlist their help in searching for lost things? Lori, from Northern California likes to pray, "Lord, have the angels put it somewhere I can find it." Here is her finder's story:

> *We were leaving on vacation, and I wanted to find my husband's sunglasses. They had been gone for weeks, and I prayed, "Heavenly Father, if you want my husband to have his sun glasses before we go on vacation, have the angels put them somewhere we can find them." I left my prayer group and went to the location we were preparing to leave from. As I opened the car door, the sunglasses were sitting on the front passenger seat of the car*

that I drive every day. They had been missing for weeks.

Lori believes the angels put them right on the seat where she could find them. Why not? Is that a wilder thought than angels breaking people out of prison or bringing them food? Stories of angelic intervention are common, yet they may seem extraordinary to our natural thinking. One angel retrieval story from a prophet named Bobby Conner has inspired many people to believe for the return of their own lost items.[1] (If you'd like to hear Bobby's story, follow the internet link in the footnotes.) Sheila, from Malaysia, was moved by Bobby's story to ask for angelic intervention in her own situation. Here is her finder's story:

> *About three years ago, my family and I were traveling between New Zealand and Malaysia. In between our trips, I had lost a gold chain with a single diamond pendant. They were gifts from my mother who had passed away, so I was desperate to find them. I knew I had packed them because I remembered doing that. I searched our luggage, and especially my little backpack, many times. I went through every single pocket, but I did not find the chain and pendant. Remembering the testimony of Bobby Conner demanding his lost knife back, I decided that I am going to do the same. God*

loves me as much as He loves Bobby. If He can do it for Bobby, God can help me find my gold chain and pendant. I did prayer for my angels to fetch them back for me no matter where they had gone. I continued to search my bags and kept asking God to send His angels to find them. Well, I could not believe my eyes when I found them in one of the pockets in my small backpack since I had searched the same place many times. God is amazing!

Testimonies are a powerful way to build our faith. The stories of other believers build faith and release prophetic grace for us to experience similar things. Odessa, from Puerto Rico, had recently heard a testimony from a leader who had recovered a lost item. This testimony led to her own story of believing for angelic help.

> *For two weeks, I couldn't find my sunglasses. I knew I had lost them during a field trip on the other side of the island. It wasn't about a fashion statement. I needed these sunglasses. Imagine humid, sticky Puerto Rico in the 90's. So, I knew I was going to an outdoor event which would be scorching hot. I then remembered the testimony. I thought to myself, "I wonder if that would work for me? Would it be ok for me to say that type of prayer?" (I was new to the Lord at the time and it all seemed a bit "woo woo.") "Would*

angels partner with me?" I wondered. "If so, why over sunglasses?" Then, this thought invaded me, "Because God loves me, even the details matter."

So, I said the prayer and praised God. I prayed that God would send angels to the specific moment, day, and time that the sunglasses were lost and to have them returned to me. I praised and thanked Him in advance. Nothing seemed to happen until I went to do my makeup. I brushed my hair into a ponytail. Put on a cap. Put on my sneakers and went towards the door. As I was walking my shoelace became untied. When I bent down to tie my sneakers, the sunglasses slid over me as if falling off my head! But wait! They weren't there when I did my makeup, brushed my hair, put on the cap? The angels delivered.

There is a lot of controversy surrounding our interaction with angels. People question whether it is okay to talk to them. Are we supposed to command them? Can we commission them? We know angels are not to be worshipped or to be our focus; but on the other hand, is it right to ignore them? Is it right to fail to employ those sent to partner with us? What can we do? There are multiple books written to answer these questions. For our purposes right now, here are a couple of ideas you can try.

. . .

ACTIVATE Angels

1. INVITE ANGELIC HELP. If you are comfortable addressing an angel, then simply ask for help. "The angel of the Lord encamps around those who fear Him." (Psalm 34:7) You could ask the angel something like this, "As a fellow servant of the Lord, would you help me find my lost item and put it in a place I can easily find it?"

2. CALL ON THE LORD OF HOSTS. If you are uncomfortable addressing an angel directly, you can still appeal to the Lord of Hosts. Jesus is the commander of the angel army. That exact title—Lord of Hosts—is used over 200 times in scripture.

Appeal to the Lord of Hosts on behalf of your lost thing: "Lord of Hosts, I am coming to you as commander of the angel army. Will you enlist your angelic servants to help me find this lost item? Please have the angels put it where I can easily find it."

3. PRACTICE THANKSGIVING. While worship of an angel is not appropriate, we can give praise and thanks to the Lord and appreciate His hosts for their assistance in finding our lost thing.

12
TEAMWORK

ONE OF THE MANY benefits of having friends who are believers is that we all have different specialties and differing levels of faith for certain gifts. When we put our specialties together, we can function at higher levels of accuracy. Your friends can be eyes and ears to what you are feeling or sensing in a way that confirms your impressions or speaks to blind spots. In this way, we function like a whole body rather than a single part. Paul talks about this in his letter to the Corinthian church.

> 1 Corinthians 12:17
> If the whole body were an eye, where would the sense of hearing be? If the whole body were an ear, where would the sense of smell be?

In our organized FINDERS group that searches for missing people using prophetic impressions, we use the power of the body in a variation of the double-blind study method to determine high-priority data. What does all that mean? Often used in the medical field, double-blind studies are designed to eliminate bias and the power of suggestion. When this method is applied to finding a lost item, we ask several individuals to share their impressions on where the lost item is. We cross-reference the impressions to find those clues that are common among two or three people. The common impressions are compiled and receive a higher priority than single impressions do. For instance, if three friends mention something about your car, then that would be a high-priority search zone. If two people mentioned your backyard, then that would be our next search zone. The idea is based upon a similar scriptural principle that "every matter must be established by the testimony of two or three witnesses." (2 Corinthians 13:1)

Rob, from Australia, used team work to find his lost item. This is his finder's story:

> *I had lost my portable Bluetooth® speaker, the new one I just got for Christmas, and I normally take it to the back shed where I have some exercise equipment so I can listen to worship music and do some training. About three days went past with me tearing the house and shed apart multiple times looking for this speaker because doing a workout with no motivating music is almost eerie. After three days, I had my home group from church*

come over, and I told them I had lost my speaker. I let them know that we would have to play music off my phone unless we pray and find the speaker, so we all began to pray. We started getting what seemed like random clues such as "It's in a dark place" and "It's near some exercise equipment." So, like detectives, we started looking for the speakers near some exercise equipment. Then another said, "It's under something heavy." As we got each clue, we narrowed the search down to my exercise shed and found my speaker under the treadmill in a dark corner. We played the worship extra loud that night.

It's great when you can gather a whole team, but perhaps you only have one friend who is a believer or only one other person who is available. No problem. We also have the promise of scripture that when two or three gather in His name, He is there with them. (Matthew 18:20) When Frances lost her pet Yorkie named Shasta, she was glad for the spiritual help of her friend Cindy. This is Francis's finder's story:

> *Monday, November 19th, my little Yorkie Shasta got out of mom's backyard while we were shopping. The police saw her running fast but couldn't catch her. A worker at the Victory Center also saw her running fast up Matthew Street toward the highway. I searched for her all night and yelled until I*

was hoarse. I also knew I was on a faith walk and continuously asked the Lord to show me where Shasta was. My brother also tried finding her. I went to bed praying and worried she was out in the cold. I woke up praying. I worshiped and prayed in the Spirit until I got the note of victory. Then I got a word that the Lord heard my cries.

So, putting works to my faith, Tuesday I notified everyone possible and even had the local radio announce her missing. Then I rode around Yorktown again, hoping I'd spot her. I also drove all the way past Mercury Blvd. to look at the regional pound and fill out a missing dog application. After returning and looking again, I felt led to text Cindy, my prayer sister, and ask her for a word. We do prayer walks together at school.

She replied, "She will be found safe, keep looking. You are to witness as you go." I had the word "witness" the day before. So, I went to the street closest to where she was last seen and went door-to-door knocking. One man admitted he didn't believe in Jesus, and I prayed for him. I know he will meet me in heaven one day as seeds were planted for his soul. I had also gone to several businesses at the beach, leaving my name and number. Then, Cindy had sent me another text, "She will be out there and come back to you right where you saw her first time."

When I went out to look for Shasta that afternoon for the last time, Holy Spirit prompted me to go back to the room and get her leash. So, I took her leash and walked under the bridge on the sidewalk and yelled and yelled for Shasta up the hill in the woods. As I was looking at the dark sky, knowing it was going to be cold that night, I continued to yell. Then after a while, I heard the quiet still voice say, "I'm going to answer your cries." I looked up and Shasta appeared at the top of the hill. She came right to me and showered me with kisses. I can't explain the joy and relief that flooded me.

Another reason it can be helpful to enlist friends in the search is because we don't always have the confidence that we can clearly hear the voice of God for ourselves. Sometimes you are too distraught or emotional to focus or hear clearly. Perhaps, you are new to hearing or recognizing the voice of God. That was the situation for our next finder's story. Jen had often heard her grandmother say that God spoke to her, but when she lost her neighbor's Great Dane, she had the first-hand opportunity to put Grandma's hearing skills to the test.

I was dog-sitting for a friend who was out of town for Christmas. I wanted to go see my family, so I decided to take the dog with me. When I got to my grandma's place, I was trying to get the huge Great Dane out of my car. The dog pushed past me and ran away. I was panicked because we were far from my friend's house, and I knew the dog wouldn't be able to find his way home. I started driving around looking for the dog and spent quite a bit of time. Just when I was about to give up, I decided to call my grandma and ask her what to do. She always told us that God spoke to her, but, honestly, we just thought she was crazy. However, I was desperate to get this dog back. As I drove, Grandma told me where to turn in step-by-step directions. All of a sudden, she told me to stop right in the middle of the road. She told me to wait and shortly after, that darn dog walked right up to my car. It was about 2 miles away from where he had escaped. Now, all these years later, I hear God's voice for myself, but I will never forget that experience because it helped shape my belief that hearing from God was possible.

Teamwork can make the dream of finding your lost item a reality.

ACTIVATE Teamwork

1. CALL A FRIEND. Contact a friend or friends and ask them to pray about where your lost item can be

located.

2. RECORD YOUR IMPRESSIONS. Ask your friends to write down or record any impressions, imaginations, thoughts, or leadings of Holy Spirit they experience.

3. SHARE YOUR IMPRESSIONS. The next step is better done in person, but you can also do it over the phone or online. Get into a group and have each person share their impressions. For example, the first person might say, "I had an impression of your keys falling under a seat cushion. Did anyone else have something similar?" The rest of the group would respond positive or negative. Each person acknowledges impressions that were common and reads their unique insights.

4. SORT THE DATA. Any impressions experienced by two or more persons would go on the high-priority search list. Then, go look together for the lost item based upon the data from your session with friends.

This can be a lot of fun. It can literally be a search "party" where you enjoy watching, praying, and seeking the Lord and the lost item together.

13
DREAM OR NIGHT VISION

MODERN WESTERN CULTURE doesn't usually place great value on dreams and visions as a form of communication. As a result, many persons dismiss dreams and visions as unreal figments irrelevant to the important concerns of daily life. Conversely, in many eastern and tribal cultures, dreams are viewed as a means of supernatural communication and even as a space for action beyond waking life. The Bible was written in the context of a middle eastern culture with a high value for dreams and visions. There are at least twenty-one recorded dreams in the Bible, and each of them was considered a credible source of information and direction for spiritual intelligence requiring active follow-up on the part of the dreamer. Joseph, the stepfather of Jesus, was led by dreams.

> Matthew 2:13-15
> When they (the Magi) had gone, an angel of the Lord appeared to Joseph in a dream," Get up,"

> he said, "Take the child and his mother and escape to Egypt. Stay there until I tell you, for Herod is going to search for the child to kill him. So he got up, took the child and his mother during the night and left for Egypt, where he stayed until the death of Herod. And so was fulfilled what the Lord had said through the prophet: "Out of Egypt I called my son."

The angel kept his promise and returned in another dream to instruct Joseph when it was time to return.

> Matthew 2:18-21
> After Herod died, an angel of the Lord appeared in a dream to Joseph in Egypt and said, "Get up, take the child and his mother and go to the land of Israel, for those who were trying to take the child's life are dead." So he got up, took the child and his mother and went to the land of Israel.

Of the twenty-one recorded dreams in the bible, eleven were symbolic dreams that required interpretation. (Genesis 28:12, 37:1-10, 40, 41, Judges 7:13, Daniel 2, 4, 7) Nine of the dreams were a direct message from the Lord or an angel. (Genesis 20, 31:10-11, 31:24, 1 Kings 3:5-15, Matthew 1:18-24, 2) One dream could be considered a processing dream. (Matthew 27:19) In each of these cases, divine information and direction came through the vehicle of a dream.

To try to conceptualize the value of the potential of communication during sleep, consider that the average person will spend over 229,000 hours or 26 years (which is roughly one-third of the average life) sleeping. To fail to acknowledge the power of dreams and visions is to shut down one third of your time and life force. This choice could be compared to the equivalent of voluntarily cutting off an arm or poking out an eye; you are severely limiting your perceptions. Furthermore, visions and dreams are part of the prophetic equation promised in the outpouring of the Spirit upon all flesh.

> Joel 2:28
> And afterward, I will pour out my Spirit on all people. Your sons and daughters will prophesy, your old men will dream dreams, your young men will see visions.

All that to say that dreams and visions can be helpful and important tools in the process of finding lost things. Consider when Rhea's family lost their car keys for an entire year.

> *We lost our car keys. For a year we couldn't find them. We lived in the country at the time, and it would cost hundreds of dollars for someone to come and make another key. We prayed and prayed. One night, God gave me a dream showing me that it was under the seat of our van. (We had checked that location*

> *several times.) The next morning, my husband went out and found the keys exactly where God showed me in my dream.*

I can hear some of you asking, "Why did they have to pray so long and wait one year before the dream came?" Let's not miss the point—the exact location came in the form of a dream. Dream states are helpful places to bypass our conscious boundaries or preconceived ways of thinking. As I shared earlier in this book, your brain spends a lot of time filtering out information and stimuli that it considers unnecessary. That is why dreaming and the state in-between sleeping and waking are such revelatory zones. In this state, your brain can bypass some of the filtering systems it ordinarily uses, making you more open to new revelation and ideas. The Information Processing Theory[1] on why we dream suggests that dreams may also provide a safe place to process information and sort the clutter by cataloging thoughts and thus making room for new ideas. Regardless of why and how it happens, we know that dreams have been great detectives in solving the mysteries of missing things.

ACTIVATE Dreams

1. MAKE A DECLARATION WITH THANKSGIVING. Before you go to sleep, thank the Lord that He knows all things.

2. INVITE THE LORD INTO YOUR DREAM LIFE. Declare that God is the revealer of mysteries and invite Him to speak to you in dreams and visions of the night.

3. PREPARE TO RECEIVE. Keep a pen and paper or a recording device near your bed to capture any revelations or dreams that happen while you are sleeping or during the in-between place of waking and sleeping.

14

MAPPING METHODS

IN THIS SHORT CHAPTER, we will use a combination of the skills we have already learned combined with a map as a physical trigger. If the item that is missing falls within a larger search area, you may want to experiment with a mapping method for finding it.

Though there are no specific mapping methods of finding lost things listed in the Bible, many people in scripture were led by specific directions from Holy Spirit. Joshua's spies were sent out to explore the land and "map it out." (Joshua 18:4 NLT) Three times in the Book of Ezekiel, God asked the prophet to make a map as a part of conveying a prophetic revelation. (Ezekiel 4:1, 5:2, and 21:19)

In the same way, while searching for lost things, a map can be a helpful tool for God to initiate spiritual perceptions. The map forms a connection point between heaven and earth and becomes a trigger or catalyst for deeper revelation.

On one occasion, my team and I were able to help locate a missing child by using mapping data to pinpoint a location. Here is one my finder's stories:

> *A police officer in our church came asking for help with finding a missing child. One of our team members saw a vision flash of a street sign that began with the letter "J" and a green house. She believed that the people who had the child were considered friends of the family. When the officer questioned the family of the missing child to see if they knew anyone who lived in a green house on a street that began with "J," the family responded immediately. The police went to the green house on Jefferson Street, and the child was immediately safely recovered.*

Although a physical map was not used in this case, you can see that because the police received information about a green house on a street beginning with the letter "J," the next logical step would be to consult a map to see what streets begin with that letter. The information offered would at the very least narrow the search field. In this case, the parents knew the location based upon the description.

Some members of our FINDERS team have been able to give helpful longitude and latitude coordinates for locating missing or kidnapped people or for finding specific locations of security threats. The same thing can happen when searching for lost items. Pay attention to the slightest impressions of God speaking to your thoughts, your heart, or your physical ears and then check a map to narrow your search area.

We often practice finding methods by hiding things for our team to find. In one of these trainings, we were looking for a "lost" white Toyota Corolla sedan that one of our leaders had parked in a specific location. We passed out maps of the city to everyone in the training. They were asked to listen for clues about the make and color of the car and where it was located.

Twenty percent of the class were able to identify either the make or the general location of the car down to an easily searchable field. Several students heard the word "school" and then consulted the map to see what schools were in the search area. There were 17 schools within the search area. They were able to narrow it down to the particular elementary school parking lot where the "missing" car had been parked.

Prophetic impressions often unfold from general to specific information, and a map can be a helpful tool for clarity.

Training your senses to pick up spiritual information is a mark of maturity that often comes through practice. (Hebrews 5:14) Don't be afraid to practice with friends and family members hiding and locating items to sharpen your prophetic perceptions.

. . .

ACTIVATE Maps

Use the finding methods we have already discussed in combination with a map to locate lost items. Any of these methods can be helpful in narrowing a large search field down to a specific location.

1. USE THE SEEING METHOD. Unfold a relevant map in front of you or look up a relevant map on the internet and print it. Using the seeing method described in chapter eight, pay attention to any locations that catch your eye. Ask Holy Spirit appropriate questions in order to gather deeper and more specific details about the locations you are drawn to.

As in my "J" street example, a variation of the seeing method is when God shows you a picture of something in your mind or imagination and then you go to a map to find the picture you saw. Perhaps you see a picture of a park. You can then look up the locations of parks on a map and search for accompanying pictures on the internet that might match what you saw in the vision or imagination.

2. USE THE HEARING METHOD. Unfold a relevant map in front of you or look up a relevant map on the internet and print it. Using the hearing method described in chapter seven, listen for directions from Holy Spirit. You might hear Him say, "Put your finger down right there." You might hear coordinates or quadrants. Whatever you hear, use the map to pinpoint clues you receive.

3. Use the sensing method. Spread a map out in front of you. Using the feeling method described in chapter six, pass your hand over each quadrant of the map. Wait for a sense of heaviness, lightness, heat, cold, electricity, or tingling in your hands. Stop anywhere that the sensation changes in your hands and ask Holy Spirit for further details.

4. Use the team method. Using maps can be a fun way to involve multiple people in your search. Compare impressions between different team members to form higher priority data as described in chapter twelve.

15
MYSTICAL METHODS

Elisha was an amazing character of the seventh century BC. Among his miracles were raising the dead, healing a leper, multiplying oil and food, curing a poisonous pot of stew, finding lost things, and vividly seeing into the spirit realm. This last one—vividly seeing into the spirit realm—forms a fascinating study of a mystical finder's skill worth further examination. Let's look at the Book of 2 Kings for a better understanding of Elisha's ability to see into the spirit realm.

> 2 Kings 6:8-12
> When the king of Aram was at war with Israel, he would confer with his officers and say, "We will mobilize our forces at such and such a place." But immediately Elisha, the man of God, would warn the king of Israel, "Do not go near that place, for the Arameans are planning to mobilize their troops there." So the king of

> Israel would send word to the place indicated by the man of God. Time and again Elisha warned the king so that he would be on the alert there. The king of Aram became very upset over this. He called his officers together and demanded, "Which of you is the traitor? Who has been informing the king of Israel of my plans?" "It's not us, my lord the king," one of the officers replied. "Elisha, the prophet in Israel, tells the king of Israel even the words you speak in the privacy of your bedroom!"

This biblical account show's Elisha's ability to have an accurate awareness of events happening in a location outside the location of his physical body. We know from later text in this same chapter that Elisha possessed the ability to physically see angels and chariots in the spirit realm. (verses 16-17) In the previous chapter of 2 Kings—chapter five—we have the account of Elisha knowing a conversation spoken by his servant Gehazi and the Aramean captain Naaman without physically being present. Elisha gave his servant a chance to confess what he had done, but Gehazi lied. Let's pick up the story here in verse 26:

> 2 Kings 5:26
> But Elisha said to him, "Was not my spirit with you when the man got down from his chariot to meet you? Is this the time to take money or to accept clothes—or olive groves and vineyards, or flocks and herds, or male and female slaves?"

FINDING LOST THINGS

Let's focus on how Elisha knew the spiritual information. In this case, the prophet said, "Was not my spirit with you…?" These are mysterious words, but in the same way that God is not limited to a physical body, the spirit of a person is not entirely limited to the location of their physical self. Elisha's spirit man was able to see and perceive details of situations and conversations outside of his own physical location in both these biblical accounts. I know it sounds weird, but it's actually somewhat of a common experience in the Bible to possess awareness outside of the physical body.

The apostle Paul experienced a similar reality which he described in this way, "And I know a man—whether in the body or apart from the body I do not know, but God knows—who was caught up to paradise and heard inexpressible things, things that no one is permitted to tell." (2 Corinthians 12:3-4) Ezekiel the prophet also experienced many occasions of his spirit being taken outside of his body and gaining an awareness of conversations and events in other physical locations. (Ezekiel 11:1-13, 24-25, 40)

You might be wondering at this point, "Yeah, but does that kind of thing still happen today? Can people have remote awareness outside of their physical body?" Here is a mysterious personal account of finding a lost item that comes from a trusted member of our prophetic community:

> *I have a friend who called me to help her find a family heirloom she seemed to have lost. I had never been to her house or seen this item but said, "Sure I can ask God to help." The lost item was a credit card size photo of her grandma with a real silver picture frame. It normally lived on the makeup dresser she also had as a gift from her grandma. The desk was a hand-crafted timber with a central mirror and matching chair and had drawers on one side and an open deck for a chair to slide under.*
>
> *As I began to pray, I felt as if I, myself, were this picture. I was in my normal body, aware of everything around me, but I also felt I was this picture and that I was on the carpet facing up. As the picture, I was somewhere dark but could see a slither of light. As I was speaking to my friend, she was walking around her house. I began hearing her voice not just on the phone but as this picture. From that vantage point, the volume of her voice was changing as she walked around. As she approached her grandma's dresser, I saw her shadow pass by the small slither of light I could see. I told her to walk back slowly and when she covered the light I said, "I am right there. Can you see me?" She said, "No, the only thing in this room is this dresser." Because I felt I as the picture was on the*

carpet, I advised her to move the dresser and look behind it. She moved it left and right. All the while, I could see and hear the moving, but she could not find the photo.

Then, I heard in my ear a loud far-away voice say, "Pull out the drawer." So she pulled out the bottom drawer, and there underneath was her grandmother's photo. It kept moving because the sides of the drawers kept it hidden, and it moved whenever she moved the dresser. It was not until she opened the drawer that she was able to find the picture. God is amazing.

I know this finder's story will be a faith stretch for many people. Some might even be offended or label it a promotion of some type of new age practice. Let me assure that is not the case. I have chosen to include it in this book because it is, after all, a good example of what we are highlighting in this chapter—supernatural ways of finding lost things. I believe there is enough biblical and historical evidence for non-local perceptions that we should not deny or overlook its existence. Rather, we should embrace this truth as one of the benefits of being created in His image and of being made partakers of His divine nature. (Genesis 1:26, 2 Peter 1:4) Truth is only a treasure when it is reconciled to the person of Jesus Christ. (Colossians 2:3) My goal is not to have persons seeking weird experiences but to know all the treasures of wisdom and knowledge hidden in the person of our Lord Jesus Christ. He is the ever-present help in times of trouble. (Psalm 46:1) He is the ultimate finder.

So, how might we safely access this mystical ability for non-local awareness without concern of demonic intervention, deception, or self-motivated astral projection? I believe the key to safe access of this mystical realm starts with securing your connection. For example, when we first started using credit cards online, there was a great danger of identity and account theft. As the technology became more popular and common, software engineers designed safety protocols that guaranteed a secure connection. In a similar way, I believe that seeking and acknowledging the Lord in your exploration of the mystical secures your connection in the supernatural from invasion and theft. The following verses sound to me like God's secure connection guarantee.

> Luke 11:11-13
> Which of you fathers, if your son asks for a fish, will give him a snake instead? Or if he asks for an egg, will give him a scorpion? If you then, though you are evil, know how to give good gifts to your children, how much more will your Father in heaven give the Holy Spirit to those who ask him!

Confident in this principle after years of practice, I believe that when we ask God for Holy Spirit intelligence and interaction, God Himself secures that connection. He won't allow you to get a stone for bread, a snake for a fish, or a scorpion for an egg. He won't allow your connection to be hacked by the devil. When you stand on the foundation of what we have seen in the Bible concerning these mystical tools, and when you lean on the character and nature of God and are seeking Him and His glory, you should feel safe in pursuing supernatural tech support or Holy Spirit leading. If fear persists, it might be important to ask yourself, "Is my trust in the Father's provision and protection bigger than my fear of satan's deception?"

ACTIVATE the Mystical

1. ACKNOWLEDGE GOD. Acknowledge that God's word and substance is what holds the universe together. (Colossians 1:17) It might sound something like this, "God I believe that You created everything in the visible and invisible realm. I believe it is by You and the power of Your word that all things hold together."

2. ASK FOR THE LEADING OF HOLY SPIRIT. Acknowledge your divine union with God through the sacrifice of Christ by the power of His Holy Spirit. You may say something like, "Father, I know You are not limited to time or space. Your presence is everywhere, and You know all things. I also know that You have said that I am in You and You are in me. I ask for safe access to information outside of my limited physical location. Protect me and guide me by Your goodness." It helps to

meditate on scriptures that remind you that Christ is truly in you. (Romans 6:11, 8:9-11, Colossians 1:27, 2:6, 3:3.)

3. ENGAGE YOUR IMAGINATION. Now, keeping Christ in the process, imagine you are the lost item and see if you can perceive your location. If at any time this exercise starts feeling inappropriate, then immediately stop and worship the Lord. I realize that this mystical method will not be comfortable for everyone nor a primary skill for most, but I also know that it can be a vital key for finding lost items. This method should only be approached in full union with and awareness of the presence of Jesus Christ.

16
3RD HEAVEN SEEKING

Continuing with our more mystical search methods, I am reminded that often when looking for something it is helpful to change your vantage point. Get down on the floor and look under furniture or stand at the top of the stairway and look over the entire room. The Merriam-Webster Dictionary defines "vantage point" as "a position or standpoint from which something is viewed or considered."[1] One might say, "You can see the whole valley from the vantage point of this high hill." Dictionary.com gives this definition: "a position or place that affords a wide or advantageous perspective; viewpoint."[2] In your search for your lost item, have you accessed an advantageous perspective? Have you found a helpful vantage point? I'm speaking of your position of being seated in heavenly places in Christ Jesus.

Paul writes about this position to the believers of the ancient Ephesian church.

> Ephesians 2:6
> And God raised us up with Christ and seated us with him in the heavenly realms in Christ Jesus.

If this were just a one-off metaphoric concept, we might have reason to dismiss it. But we also see this same idea conveyed in the letter to the Colossians. Here, we see the same vantage point of being raised up together with Christ but also the admonition to feel and think from that position.

> Colossians 3:1-3
> Since, then, you have been raised with Christ, set your hearts on things above, where Christ is, seated at the right hand of God. Set your minds on things above, not on earthly things. For you died, and your life is now hidden with Christ in God.

What does your search look like from the greatest vantage point in the universe? You are truly seated with Christ in heavenly places. You can see everything from there. That vantage point is a great place to begin the search for your missing item. Davina found herself under a physical attack that she believed had a spiritual root. When she couldn't find the source, she invited Holy Spirit to reveal how He saw things. This is her unique finder's story:

> *A few years ago, I had been having some physical attack with sickness, and I was*

asking the Lord if there was any sin in my life or anything in my home that may have opened the door to the enemy and given him a foothold. The Lord led me to have a clear out of my unit.[3] *I closed my eyes and asked Him to show me in my mind. In the dark, He led me into each room, one-by-one. In a few rooms I saw white glowing areas that He highlighted to me. I opened my eyes and went to those locations; and in those exact spots, I found something that was a bit questionable. I threw those things out and my health improved after that!*

This is a unique finder's story because Davina was trying to find spiritual entry points that might be affecting her health. Not every sickness has a direct access point through sin or a demonic gateway, but I have personally witnessed both deliverances and healings that were related to the physical removal of certain objects in a room. Davina's story reminds me of the prayer of King David.

Psalm 139:23-24
Search me, God, and know my heart; test me
and know my anxious thoughts. See if there is
any offensive way in me and lead me in the way
everlasting.

Though Davina's story is about finding a spiritual source that needed to be removed, I believe the same vantage point of being seated in heavenly places with Christ Jesus can be used to find any item that is lost. Seeing how God sees can be a key to many things, but it is certainly helpful in the realm of finders.

ACTIVATE Vantage Point

1. FIX YOUR EYES. Close your eyes and focus inwardly on the reality of being seated in heavenly places in and with Christ Jesus.

2. SET YOUR HEART. Make a heart connection with that reality. Enjoy the warm glow of His love and the absolute peace and joy emanating from that favored position.

3. LOOK FROM THIS VANTAGE POINT. After you are firmly aware of this reality, open your spiritual eyes from this vantage point and look for your lost thing.

17
PERSEVERANCE AND VARIANCE OF METHODS

One of the greatest challenges in finding lost things is wrestling with faith and patience. It seems like supernatural and spiritual insight should always produce instantaneous results, but that is not how it works every time. Prophetic perceptions often speak of an end result or promise, not always the process or timing between the challenge and the resolution. We see this truth clearly in the 2,600-year-old writings of the prophet Habakkuk.

> Habakkuk 2:3
> For the revelation awaits an appointed time; it speaks of the end and will not prove false. Though it linger, wait for it; it will certainly come and will not delay.

The revelation will not prove false. But why the waiting game? Some believe that God in His sovereignty has scripted out every detail on an exact time line and that we as mere humans must wait for our role or script to be queued by the Great Director for each part of His plan to be played out in its proper time. Certainly, God knows the perfect timing for everything, and times and seasons are in His hands. Yet we see across the entire record of scripture that some things have a perfect time and other things are movable and shapeable in time.

Because God's value is relationship, His methodology is partnership. He loves to partner with us in time and process. Perhaps that is because God's end game is not always the result or function of our specific request but the life qualities the process produces within us to create a more abundant outcome. We are trying to find lost house keys, and the Father is shaping formerly lost sons and daughters into extraordinary world changers. Sometimes those two things overlap in time and, at other times, they do not. Still, wrestling with faith and perseverance always produces a better outcome in us as promised in the writings of James, the brother of Jesus.

> James 1:3-4
> Because you know that the testing of your faith
> produces perseverance. Let perseverance finish
> its work so that you may be mature and
> complete, not lacking anything.

Emory experienced first-hand the testing of her faith and the result of the perseverance it produced. Here is her finder's story.

> *Several years ago, I was new to fully walking in the Holy Spirit and was working for an accounting firm that served high net worth clients. One of our jobs was to assist with opening new bank accounts and securing debit cards on behalf of our clients. We followed a strict policy and procedure in how these cards were obtained, secured, and delivered to the client. One day a client notified me they were en route to pick up their new card and would arrive in 30 minutes. When I went to our safe to get the card, it wasn't in the appropriate location. I searched every safe we used in case it had been misfiled, but to no avail. I returned to the office and shared with a few of the staff that the card was missing. We were all concerned, but then I said, "God knows where it is, and I'm going to ask Him to show me where to find it!"*

I went to our storage room, closed the door, and prayed, asking Holy Spirit where to look. I heard Him tell me it was in the pedestal of a fellow employee's desk. The employee was out sick that day, so I searched the drawer, but there was no card. I figured I'd heard incorrectly, so I went back to the storage room, sat in the quiet, and asked again! He said, "It's in the pedestal."

"But I looked and didn't see it!" I said.

> *"Look again!" He nudged.*
>
> *I went back, pulled out every file folder and document in the pedestal and still didn't find the card. Disheartened, but confident in God's ability to come through, I went back to the storage room one more time. At this point, I had less than ten minutes before the client arrived to pick up the missing debit card.*
>
> *"It's in the pedestal."*
>
> *A light bulb went off in my mind...He didn't say it was in a drawer, He said in the pedestal!*
>
> *I returned to the desk and removed the drawers from the pedestal and there was the debit card—stuck in between the drawers!*

Faith and perseverance are always producing something. If not your immediate desired outcome of finding, they are still working behind the scenes. Even the great heroes of faith throughout history had to wrestle with believing to the end. The need for perseverance is not an indicator that God doesn't want your outcome to be fully realized. Quite the opposite is true. Look at this great promise from the ancient letter to the Hebrew church.

> Hebrews 6:11-12
> We want each of you to show this same diligence to the very end, so that what you hope for may be fully realized. We do not want you to

become lazy, but to imitate those who through faith and patience inherit what has been promised.

The context of this verse is certainly salvation and heaven, but a consistent principle throughout scripture and this book has been that God truly cares about what you care about. He invites us to ask for whatever we will on many occasions and promises a positive outcome. (Matthew 21:22, Mark 11:24, John 14:13, 15:7,16) I'm certainly not saying that we always get everything we ask for. The point is that perseverance and faith are partners in achieving what can seem like an impossible outcome. In compiling this book, I received many great finder's stories from online friends around the world who showed diligence and faith to the very end. Their hope was fully realized months and even years later, but it happened. Faith and perseverance together produced a hope realized. Bri, a teenager from Minnesota, discovered this truth when she lost a precious ring her father had given her. This is her finder's story:

> *We wanted to share the story of Bri losing her purity ring that her dad gave her when she turned sixteen. One day coming home from school, she fell in the snow and her ring came off. She looked everywhere in the snow and was so devastated that she lost something so precious. We prayed and asked God to please keep others from finding it and to bring angels*

> *to help us find it. Bri was so sad when it didn't show up; we were all discouraged. She walked the same path every day to school and never saw it. Three months later, Bri was walking to school and saw the ring in the middle of the sidewalk just sitting there completely clean and in perfect condition. She ran home, and we had a praise party. It was so cool and such a faith builder to all of us that God can do anything!*

Three months of not finding something precious can seem like an eternity to anyone but especially a teenager. Discouragement and disillusionment may come like a passing storm but hold on to faith. Speak His peace over your storm and hold on. Never giving up is a key to finding. Faith is always worth embracing. Faith pleases God; faith and patience are virtues producing a family resemblance that the Father wants to see in all His children.

Gina held on to hope for ten years when she lost one earring from a precious set that her mom had given her. This is Gina's finder's story:

> *Shortly after I moved into my house in 2009, I lost an earring. It disappeared almost like out of nowhere which always bothered me. I remember praying and asking the Lord to help me find it. It just seemed so mysterious how it disappeared. After about ten years of never*

finding it, I considered getting rid of the one that remained but couldn't do it. They were special to me, white gold earrings my mom bought for me as a gift in high school.

In February of 2019, while gutting my basement and bathroom downstairs, we were tearing up the flooring. I noticed the earring sitting on something in the construction zone. Puzzled, I asked my dad who was helping me, "Where did this come from?" He said, "Oh, that was under the old flooring. I just found it." He didn't realize that it was my earring. It was pretty amazing that God cared enough to return that earring all those years later.

The funny thing is the flooring that the earring was underneath was laid before I moved in. So, it's not even explainable in the natural for it to have been buried under there. Totally a miracle.

I always believed the Lord would return it, so I held on to the other one. It was just so amazing that it took almost ten years and showed up when and where I least expected it.

What do you do when you have tried all these finder methods and still have not found what you are looking for? You persevere.

. . .

ACTIVATE Perseverance

1. PERSEVERE. Hold on to faith with perseverance. When it looks like nothing is happening, make a declaration of trust: "Something is always happening! I trust that you are doing things right now in answer to my asking and seeking. Lord, I know you are working behind the scenes to make all things beautiful in their time. (Ecclesiastes 3:11) Everyone who asks receives and those who seek find. (Matthew 7:7) In your Name, I am a finder."

2. EXPERIMENT. Try various finding methods. One of the reasons I put so many finder's methods in this book is so that you could see the many ways that God moves and speaks to us. Enjoy the journey of seeking by experimenting with different methods of partnering with God in the finding process.

3. GIVE THANKS. Season your petitions with thanksgivings. The word most partnered with the subject of prayer in the Bible is different forms of "thanks." Thanksgiving opens gates. (Psalm 100:4) Always present petitions with acknowledgement of things you are thankful for. Your prayer might sound something like this: "Father, thank you that You know all things. Thank you that You care about what I care about because You care for me. Help me find my lost item from this position of gratitude for all You have already done and for what You are about to do."

18
THE ETHICS OF SEARCHING

ONCE A PERSON BECOMES KNOWN AS A "FINDER," other people who have lost things will begin to seek them out. People often interpret testimonies as an announcement of identification of a unique or specialized anointing or gift. If you recognize that you have a special grace in one or more areas of finding lost things, there are some ethics or points of etiquette I recommend. This is by no means meant to be comprehensive but rather a simple introduction to some important ethnics of searching I have discovered through the years.

First, watch your language. Beware of presumptuous or well-meaning statements. Don't make a promise that you can't keep. If you are searching on behalf of someone else, it is not usually wise to promise that you will locate what is lost. Sometimes people say such things as a means of comfort, but it is better to say something like "We will ask the Lord and do everything within our ability to help you." This first principle of etiquette is similar to what we see in the writings of James.

> James 4:13-16
> Now listen, you who say, "Today or tomorrow we will go to this or that city, spend a year there, carry on business and make money." Why, you do not even know what will happen tomorrow. What is your life? You are a mist that appears for a little while and then vanishes. Instead, you ought to say, "If it is the Lord's will, we will live and do this or that." As it is, you boast in your arrogant schemes. All such boasting is evil.

Many truths in the Bible are held in the tension between two seeming paradoxes. In other words, sometimes the Bible often presents what seems to be two opposite truths. For instance, Proverbs 26:4-5 says, "Do not answer a fool according to his folly, or you yourself will be just like him. Answer a fool according to his folly, or he will be wise in his own eyes." Wait a minute. Am I supposed to answer a fool according to his folly or not answer him that way? The answer is yes. The truth will be found by examining two seemingly opposite ideas. It is like verifying the authenticity of a precious coin by clearly inspecting its opposite sides. Nevertheless, there are times when a gift of faith or a heavenly surety comes upon you making it both necessary and proper to make an absolute declaration. When Saul the son of Kish was looking for his father's donkeys, the prophet Samuel made this type of declaration.

> 1 Samuel 9:20
> As for the donkeys you lost three days ago, do not worry about them; they have been found. And to whom is all the desire of Israel turned, if not to you and your whole family line?

Samuel was able to make this declaration because he had been clearly instructed by God. Maturity can measure between real faith and arrogant or untrained presumption. However, if you make a promise that doesn't come true or if you provide information that does not prove accurate, it is important to be willing to acknowledge your mistake. Apologize. Humble yourself and make right anything you need to take responsibility for. Then get back up and try again. If you are taking risks of faith, you will certainly make some mistakes and experience some failures along the way. But keep trying.

Humility and teachability are keys. My mentor used to say, "No matter how much you know, you only know a part." This idea is a principle based upon 1 Corinthians 13.

> 1 Corinthians 13:9
> For we know in part and we prophesy in part.

Remember that no matter how much you know or see through prophetic perception, you are still dealing with partial information. It's good to be confident, but it is never wise to be arrogant or to boast of things you have no real control over. Humility and gentleness are called the yoke of Jesus. (Matthew 11:29) Stay under the yoke of Christ, and the work is always easier and better.

Second, if you become known as a finder, you might have to set up some boundaries or criteria for your finding skills so that you do not get overwhelmed. Chances are you will have more requests than it would be healthy to take on. Our FINDERS organization for lost and missing children only accepts requests from direct family members of the missing child. There are many reasons for this that are beyond the purpose of this book, but I mention it only to say that there are definite boundaries and criteria for what our teams will and will not do.

You might want to consider some of the following boundaries.

CONSIDER THE TIME COMMITMENT. How much time do you have to give to finding? Don't commit to more cases than you have time or energy for. Overcommitting is a sure recipe for burnout. Don't allow yourself to be moved by need alone because there will always be an ocean of human need. If you try to save everyone, you are likely to drown yourself.

Stay within the boundaries of what you clearly have time for and feel good committing to. Jesus demonstrated boundaries in His earthly ministry and so should you. He took time to rest and to pray.

FACTOR IN YOUR CALLING. Are there special areas of finding that you have a gift, burden, or calling for? Does the request match your current skill set? Grace multiplies in areas of gifting, burden, and calling, so you are much less likely to "run out of gas" in one of these areas. For instance, you might have a specialty in the area of family heirlooms. Family might be a really important subject to you, and your passion in that area can build a special bridge for spiritual intelligence. Or you might have a specialty grace for personal items like wallets, keys, phones, and sunglasses. I know of one woman who is a veterinary specialist and has a 98 percent success rate with finding lost pets using supernatural perceptions. Others may have grace and gifting for many varied types of finding. The point is you are not being insensitive to others by setting boundaries; you are staying in your lane. Run the race that is marked out for you, and you will not grow weary. (Hebrews 12:1)

CHECK YOUR PERMISSIONS. It's also good to ask, "Do I have permission or authority to search in this area?" Don't involve yourself in someone else's search without permission or an invitation. Never involve yourself in a police case just because you have had a spiritual perception. You might get arrested for interfering or obstructing justice. Many finder's cases require permission. Not all spiritual perceptions are meant to be shared. Just because you have spiritual intel on something does not mean you have an assignment or permission to share it. Be aware that your authority and access in the Spirit is often different than your authority and favor in the natural world. Don't go places you are not invited to go. Don't offer unsolicited counsel. Ask if the person is open to spiritual input. When you operate outside of your assigned authority, you often feel unprotected and more vulnerable to attack.

WILL MONEY BE INVOLVED? This is a tough subject. Should a person accept money or reward for finding when using God-given spiritual gifts? Is this a case of "freely you have received, freely give"? (Matthew 10:8) Is it ever right to receive compensation for using a spiritual gift? It's important to remember that every gift and skill comes from the Lord. A gift for painting, music, architecture, or finances is just as much a gift of God as prophecy. We don't hesitate to pay people for these gifts. I believe there are two principles in play here. The first principle is to follow your conscience and the leading of Holy Spirit. The Bible records occasions of prophets both receiving and denying gifts or compensation for their spiritual intel.

Let's first look at some cases where people received payment. Daniel received gifts for the spiritual insights He provided for a wicked king.

Daniel 5:29
Then at Belshazzar's command, Daniel was
clothed in purple, a gold chain was placed
around his neck, and he was proclaimed the
third highest ruler in the kingdom.

Both Daniel and Joseph had multiple occasions where they were rewarded or promoted for sharing spiritual insights and intel.

We also see a pattern in scripture concerning inquiring of a prophetic specialist. One of these many instances is found in the record of 1 Samuel. When Saul the son of Kish had lost his donkeys, one of his servants suggested that they go to the man of God to inquire of the Lord. Saul could not conceive of doing so without taking some sort of gift. Here is the biblical account:

1 Samuel 9:6-8
But the servant replied, "Look, in this town
there is a man of God; he is highly respected,
and everything he says comes true. Let's go
there now. Perhaps he will tell us what way to
take." Saul said to his servant, "If we go, what
can we give the man? The food in our sacks is
gone. We have no gift to take to the man of God.
What do we have?" The servant answered him
again. "Look," he said, "I have a quarter of a
shekel of silver. I will give it to the man of God
so that he will tell us what way to take."

It appears historically that when a person went to inquire of the Lord through a specialist, they usually brought a gift.

Conversely, there are an equal number of Bible accounts where a prophet refused to accept gifts for certain types of ministry or spiritual services. Consider the case of Elisha and the healing of the Aramean commander. (2 Kings 5:16) In this account, Elisha refused to accept payment, and his servant Gehazi thought his master had made a mistake. The servant snuck out and chased down the chariot to ask for 75 pounds of silver and two sets of clothing. Naaman, the commander insisted on paying twice that much. Yet the consequences of this action on the part of Gehazi were great. The disease the commander was cured of came upon Gehazi, and he was suddenly leprous. As I said earlier in this chapter, your conscience and the leading of Holy Spirit should be your guide.

The second general principle many of our teams operate under is this: prophetic ministry is free, but prophetic consulting carries a fee. In other words, we never charge for prophetic encouragement or the spontaneous flow of the Spirit in the gift of prophecy. However, many of our team members will charge when someone comes with a request to inquire of specific spiritual counsel. In these cases, what the clients are paying for is much like a counseling or coaching session that includes supernatural insights combined with professional skills or experience.

Receiving payment for these types of professional services makes the work more of a business. Sustainability in a business requires profitability or funding of some type. You can't volunteer your services all the time if you are doing this work full time. The worker is worth his support. (Matthew 10:10)

So, should you charge or not charge? Is it ok to receive a gift or reward from a person you have served with a spiritual gift? Most people, including pastors and plumbers, receive payment for the service of their spiritual gifts every week in some form. Each person must understand the biblical principles involved and follow the leading of Holy Spirit. Don't make your standard someone else's standard. Each person must decide in their own heart what their boundaries are in this area and stay true to that leading.

The ethics related to finding are not meant to hinder you but rather to protect you. People are passionate and emotional about their lost items, and in compassion and mercy, you can get swept up in their drama. You can also have successes that push you away from faith in God to self-confidence. Hold your heart steady in the hope of Jesus Christ. Without Him, we can do nothing. (John 5:19, 30, 15:5) Our goal is that finding would be part of the ministry of reconciliation that would demonstrate God's love for the world and its people. May the supernatural skills of finding merely be a part of the light of the world that points to the one true source of light, Jesus Christ. Let us do all things to His glory. To Him be all the glory and honor and praise forever and ever.

ACTIVATE Ethics

1. BE ACCOUNTABLE. Have you made any vows in finding that caused a problem you need to apologize for? If so, go humble yourself to the person you have made presumptuous promises to. Remember the sting of wrong information, but don't let it stop you from pursuing the skills of a finder.

2. CONSIDER YOUR TIME. How much time do you have to dedicate to finding? Determine in advance what is appropriate, or you may be consumed in the case. It's really wise to set these boundaries in advance because certain cases can be emotionally stirring. Without boundaries in place, you may over-extend yourself out of emotion rather than leading.

3. SET YOUR PRIORITIES. Are there special areas of passion and grace you should prioritize? Are you mainly searching for your own items or those of friends, or do you want to be available to help strangers or engage in governmental partnerships? Make sure you are well-practiced with some solid success stories under your belt before making commitments to others.

4. KNOW YOUR PERMISSIONS. Are you operating with a sphere of authority and permission? Keep yourself safe

by staying within the boundaries of permission and invitation.

5. Know your financial conviction. It's good to decide in advance what you will do if someone offers you money or a reward. Try to think big picture and follow your heart.

19
PUTTING IT ALL TOGETHER

I HOPE YOU HAVE ENJOYED this journey and exploration of supernatural finding techniques that are a natural part of our relationship with God. I must confess that even while writing this book, I had a few frantic moments of searching for something that was "lost." That must seem odd to you, the reader. It seems that after writing the book which teaches finding techniques and receiving countless testimonies of miraculous finding stories from around the world, I would never have a problem with lost things again. Unfortunately, that's not the case for me, and it probably won't be true for you either. Finding is still a journey and a choice.

On the journey, I'm still learning to seek God's counsel and wisdom daily. I'm still growing in my ability to recognize and respond to the many ways that God speaks. I'm still practicing the ability to stop in the face of perceived loss and acknowledge that God is with me to seek and to save that which is lost. One of my goals in writing this book is that it would be a tool for increasing your friendship with God. In discovering the different methods for finding, we are also learning new ways that He speaks to us. God is always communicating, but as we have seen in the previous lessons, He speaks in diverse languages. Experiencing these different modes of communication will certainly be a journey. So, enjoy the journey. Enjoy learning and growing in the many diverse ways that God speaks and increase in your ability to recognize His voice. As you do, your trust in Him will grow and you will deepen in friendship and love.

I also said that finding skills are a choice. As a choice, I've discovered that knowing something is true does not in itself give you the power to engage that truth. You still must choose it. You must make the choice to seek first God and His kingdom in all things. Jesus said it this way:

> John 13:17
> Now that you know these things, you will be blessed if you do them.

Though the context of this passage was different, the principle is the same. The blessing of finding is not in the knowing but in the doing. Doing takes practice. Practice your simple trust. Practice childlike expectancy. Practice the ability to not stress under the tyranny of the urgent and to seek first the kingdom of God. That doesn't all happen right away.

That is why finding has been a journey for me, not a destination. Still today, I don't find everything I have lost, but I believe it is possible. I hold on to hope. I have seen many lost things and persons restored. It's part of my ever-growing and evolving relationship with God. I trust it will now be part of yours as well.

In closing, I invite you into this story of redemption that began in God's heart thousands of years ago. Remember that before He created anything in our time and space continuum, He made a way for all that was lost to be found and restored. Through Christ, you now share in the ministry and mission of restoration and reconciliation. We have shared our stories with you; now it is your turn to share His story and your story with the world. Let your light (of finding lost things and persons) so shine before men, that they will see your good works and glorify the Father who is in heaven. (Matthew 5:16, parenthesis mine)

In the future, I hope to write about our journey in finding missing persons using similar techniques. For the last several years, a team of faithful believers around the world have been using supernatural skills to find missing children, locate kidnapped victims, and reconnect lost family members. Their collective stories are truly inspiring. Though we are only in the infancy of this discovery, every story of success is a treasure of the redemptive power of Jesus Christ to restore everything and everyone that is lost.

Until I'm able to meet you again in the penning of those stories, I hope you will put these things you have learned into practice. Read over them again and meditate on the power of these testimonies. Embark on your own journey of discovery of the power to find lost things supernaturally through relationship with Jesus Christ.

NOTES

INTRODUCTION

1. "Loss." *Merriam-Webster.com Dictionary*, Merriam-Webster, https://www.merriam-webster.com/dictionary/loss. Accessed 3 Sep. 2020.

5. DIVINE RECALL

1. Wikipedia: the Free Encyclopedia, https://en.wikipedia.org/w/index.php?title=Hail_Mary_pass&oldid=968691919, July 25, 2020.

7. FINDING WITH HEARING

1. A fete is an outdoor festival, feast, party, or school carnival.

9. FINDING WITH KNOWING

1. https://www.lexico.com/en/definition/revelation. Accessed July 28, 2020.

11. ANGELS ON ASSIGNMENT

1. Bobby Conner's lost knife story as told by Bill Johnson can be heard at https://www.youtube.com/watch?v=3tNZKUl4D5E. Retrieved July 29, 2020.

13. DREAM OR NIGHT VISION

1. Vinney, Cynthia. "Information Processing Theory: Definition and Examples." ThoughtCo, Aug. 29, 2020, thoughtco.com/information-processing-theory-definition-and-examples-4797966.

16. 3RD HEAVEN SEEKING

1. "Vantage point." *Merriam-Webster.com Dictionary*, Merriam-Webster, https://www.merriam-webster.com/dictionary/vantage%20point. Accessed 10 Sep. 2020.
2. "Vantage point." Dictionary.com Unabridged, Random House, https://www.dictionary.com/browse/vantage-point. Accessed 10 Sep. 2020.
3. An Asian phrase similar in meaning to doing a thorough examination of your home.

Made in the USA
Monee, IL
15 November 2024